THE LIFE AND MISADVENTURES
OF
MIGUEL DE CERVANTES

D. Miguel de Ceruantes Saauedra

Iuan de Iaurigui Pinxit año 1600.

CERVANTES

THE LIFE AND MISADVENTURES

OF

MIGUEL DE CERVANTES

by

MARIANO TOMÁS

*Translated
from the Spanish*

by

WARRE B. WELLS

Illustrated

BOSTON AND NEW YORK

HOUGHTON MIFFLIN COMPANY

1934

Vida y Desventuras de Miguel de Cervantes,
by Mariano Tomás, was first published in
Barcelona in 1933. English translation first
published in 1934

PRINTED IN GREAT BRITAIN BY THE EDINBURGH PRESS, EDINBURGH

PREFACE

I do not know whether this *Life of Cervantes*, which I offer you here, will meet with your approval, or even whether it fulfils my own intentions.

Since it is your business, and since I must be brief, let me deal first with the matter of your approval, before I proceed to the matter of my own intentions.

If you are fond of figures and statistics; if you expect to find tax-collectors' accounts, genealogical tables and obscure family ramifications meticulously set down here, you will not like this book of mine, for you will find it lacking in any such erudition.

If you like reading *Lives* in which what may be taken as certain is hooked on to what is sheer imagination, so that the whole becomes little more than a work of fiction, you had better close this book before it bores you.

But if you are an admirer of the works of Cervantes, that man who lost the use of one hand to the greater glory of Spain; if you are interested in the adventures that really happened to him and in the sad story of his life, then, perhaps, you may read these pages of mine through to the end, lured on by your curiosity and with your interest held by the story I have to tell, rather than by the way in which I tell it.

I should have liked to say: "lured on by your curiosity *and your enthusiasm*." But the enthusiasm which went to the writing of these pages was mine, and I have no right to count upon yours. If I am wrong, and we can join

5

hands now and again, I shall reckon myself well repaid for any trouble I may have taken to arouse your enthusiasm.

You will not need to tell me about this enthusiasm of yours. I shall feel it flickering about this book of mine. I shall find this book shining more brightly in my own mind, just like slack water in the night-time which seems dull and without lustre, until, all at once, it is clad in light, because the reflection of a star has come to bathe in it.

I have filled this book of mine with quotations from Cervantes' own works, in order to make it easier for you to recall those pages of his in which he tells us about himself: those pages of his which enshrine his memory of himself, his real self, amid all the imaginary memories of him. This book of mine may be regarded as serving the purpose of a pitcher, thrust into the stream of his works. It tenders to your lips, thirsting for information about his life, the trickle which is all that one can offer to satisfy you.

I have borrowed from Cervantes' own writings such references as he makes to himself and his doings. I should have been only too glad to carry this process to such a point that I might be accused of adopting the easy course of constructing this book of mine out of bits of his. Unfortunately, however, there is not sufficient material to go to the making of any such mosaic.

And now, in the course of discussing what may meet with your approval, I have already given you a hint of my own intentions.

I have no desire to make this book of mine a work of erudition. Since figures and figuring are dull things, I spare you details of tax-gathering and casting balance-sheets; but

6

I offer you the broad outlines of these matters in so far as they affect the life of Cervantes. I deliberately pass over obscure periods in the lives of people with whom his own life came into contact; but I deal with these lives when they are so closely linked with his own that time and chance set them all travelling the same road together.

I have chosen to write not the biography of a family, as so many distinguished pens have done, but the biography of a single man: a man who, by comparison with his own family, shows us the working of Providence, which creates some people inconspicuous and others glorious, even though it may fashion them out of such similar material as the flesh and blood of parents and children and brothers and sisters.

On the other hand, I have no desire to garb this figure of Miguel de Cervantes in any other finery than the old clothes which he wore in his lifetime, and out of which the dust has been beaten by sedulous students of the truth about him.

Sometimes I have ventured to delve into his thoughts, deducing them from the landscape which presented itself to his eyes, the bitterness which preyed upon his heart, or the illumination which sprang to life in his mind and streamed on to his pages. It may be no more daring to imagine a state of mind than to assert an unproven fact; but I do not think that I have strayed very far along this path, for very often, blinded by the light to which it led, I have not dared to follow it at all.

I wished to make this book of mine neither a Blue Book nor a work of fiction, but a *Life*, and therefore to put all the emotion of life into it.

For this purpose, I sometimes paint in the horizon, the background, the minor figures which have their being and laugh and weep against that background. I feared lest, if I presented you with Cervantes' portrait against a neutral background, I might leave you with the impression of a mannered silhouette, without life or expression, like an Egyptian hieroglyphic.

But now I am afraid that this desire of mine to convey the emotion of life may have remained no more than a good intention, and that the whole picture I offer you may be drab and colourless, like those portraits of our grandparents of the past century, which present them on a balcony overlooking a garden, with a background that, instead of sky and flowers, is merely lampblack.

It is for you to say whether I have fulfilled my purpose, and to forgive me if I have made other than deliberate omissions or fallen into involuntary errors.

ILLUSTRATIONS

CERVANTES . . . . *Frontispiece*

FACING PAGE

SUPPOSED SELF-PORTRAIT OF CERVANTES   16

HOUSE WHERE CERVANTES LIVED IN VALLADOLID   96

CERVANTES IN PRISON   160

CERVANTES' HOUSE IN EL TOBOSO   176

CERVANTES MAKES HIS WILL   240

THE LIFE AND MISADVENTURES OF
MIGUEL DE CERVANTES

CHAPTER I

ON the twenty-second day of December 1569, that very worthy gentleman, the notary Duarte de Acuña—whose name, apart from this, nobody would ever remember—ordered his scrivener, Rodrigo de Vera, to issue, at the request of an interested party, a certificate of purity of blood in favour of a certain young man who was then staying in Rome, in the hope of entering the royal army in the service of His Catholic Majesty of Spain.

This young man was going on for twenty-two. All his own expectation of offspring still lay in the future. By way of immediate ancestry, all that he could boast was his father the blood-letter, a surgeon through force of circumstances rather than from any vocation or qualification, who was now so unsteady in his handling of the lancet, and so blunted in his faculties by poverty and misfortune, that the only description he could give of himself was " resident in the capital " ; and his grandfather, a man of the law, narrow-minded, hard-faced, and heavy-handed.

What Rodrigo de Cervantes, that surgeon come down in the world, presented to the very worthy notary Duarte de Acuña was no written evidence of illustrious descent, but simply living, speaking witnesses to the fact that he was well and truly married to Doña Leonor de Cortinas, and that the fruit of their union was the young man who was now in Italy. What he requested was no attestation of armorial bearings or lofty lineage, but simply a plain statement that this young man was of old Christian blood, untainted by heretics who had worn the *sambenito* or by any Moorish admixture.

When the scrivener had finished the job, the notary scribbled his signature, in complex arabesques, at the foot of the document, without running his eyes over it or casting even a glance at that unknown name, Miguel de Cervantes, quite unworthy of the waste of such a very worthy legal gentleman's precious time that would be involved in deciphering it.

Miguel de Cervantes received this document in May or June of the following year. From that moment he discarded his retainer's livery in favour of the brightly coloured tight doublet and wide breeches with which the Spanish infantry adorned itself.

By this time, in the stately, ceremonious ante-rooms of the Roman palaces, he had not found so many doors opening upon the field of his hopes as he had expected when he came to Italy in the train of the Pontifical delegate Acuaviva. By now he realised that doors closed behind purple robes and embroidered velvet mantles, without granting admittance to those who, like himself, wore the humble livery of servitors.

Perhaps in war, in which advancement and reputation were earned by doughty deeds rather than by rich attire and high-sounding name, he would achieve what he was now sure bowing and scraping would never win him : wealth and fame.

These two things he sought in any possible direction. He

was buoyed up by his assurance that, if he once found them within his reach, he would lay hands upon them so firmly that they would never escape him again. He felt certain that, some day, they were bound to be his; for he looked inside himself, in the shining mirror of his imagination, and he saw his inner self so rich, so adorned, that he was persuaded God must have created him to live in the midst of riches and adornment.

He had no bent towards war. He simply felt a vague restlessness. It foreshadowed his future greatness, but did not point out his path. He took the first path that presented itself.

While the certificate of his purity of blood was on its way from Castile, Miguel walked amid the glorious ruins of the Eternal City.

" He visited its temples, he venerated its remains, he admired its power; and, just as merely from the claws of a lion one can arrive at knowledge of its strength and ferocity, so he inferred the might of Rome from its shattered marbles, its statues maimed or whole, its broken arches and its ruined baths . . . and from its streets, whose very names bespeak authority over all the other cities of the world: the Via Appia, the Via Flaminia, the Via Julia. . . ."

This evocative power of names which he makes the pilgrim in his *Persiles* feel—Miguel had felt it himself, years before, during those days of waiting. We carry names within ourselves, tapping away at our minds; and, when we have before our eyes the shattered stones to which one of them clings, the name springs out of our minds into our hearts, and we experience in our hearts a pang such as we have never known before.

13

Many an evening Miguel must have gone to seek the solitude of the ruins. In the deep silence of the abandoned baths, in a grove of cypresses just like those beside the slender stream that waters the flower-beds, which softly make their moan today when the north wind lashes them, under the shelter of towering brown walls, he must have given free rein to his thoughts and his imagination.

The one brought him memories of events that were now behind him. The other made events that were still to come already present and glorious.

He saw himself once more amid the students at the San Ildefonso school, in his native town, the university town of Alcalá, where he had come into the world one autumnal Sunday, in a modest house not far from the parish church of Santa Maria; or larking with young rapscallions of his own age and condition beneath the porticoes of ancient Complutum, or on the banks of the Henares.

He recalled the stories he had heard from his relations about his grandfather Juan, who had been rich and powerful, and had moved about with his family from one town to another in Castile and Andalusia : fawned upon and respected as an upright judge, but so stern a one that, in the absence of the regular officers of justice, he did not hesitate to put malefactors to the torture with his own hands in order to wring confession from them.

But, above all, what stung Miguel to bitterness was the recollection of those days of hunger, when his father, already dull-witted and deaf, went from place to place in search of a clientèle which he never found; and especially of that dreadful day in Valladolid, in the year 1552, when, after his father had sold or pawned all his clothes, coffers, cushions, tapestries and trinkets, the constables came to seize what little was left to them and carry the unfortunate Rodrigo off to prison, there to expiate the crime of having tried to meet his family's needs by resort to the generosity of moneylenders and having nothing more to put into their clutches.

Perhaps these dark clouds of Miguel's memories let through a ray of silver lining at his remembrance of his aunt Maria, fair, forward, and free, who became the mistress of an archdeacon, without sullying for so small a matter the fair name of the Cervantes family, and proceeded to go to law, with the backing of the upright judge her father, for recovery of the maravedies promised when she made him a present of her virginity; and at his remembrance of his own sisters, Andrea and Magdalena, who already seemed to be the heiresses, alike in fairness and in forwardness, of Maria de Cervantes. They came to the help of the family— and doubtless would go on doing so—whenever poverty threatened, with all the resources of their brains and their beauty.

It did not pain Miguel that such should be the means by which, from time to time, fortune smiled on the Cervantes family. He felt for the girls nothing but an acquiescent affection. The times were different from our own; and if in most families, even noble familes, such little arrangements, such irregularities, were to be found, that gives us no right to pass severe judgment on customs which we do not understand, or to talk about licentiousness in connection with affairs which, in their own day, were not branded with the harsh names that we should now use.

Miguel was in no way pained; but he dreamed that some

day it would be he who would pour out over his family the horn of plenty.

His life, up to this, had leant upon the lives of those around him. It had followed the track which these other lives had marked out for it up hill and down dale: the twisting, talkative streets of Alcalá; trips to Madrid and Valladolid, with stays at dubious houses in miry alleys; the banks of the Guadalquivir, scene of his sole happy hours of childhood in the straitened circumstances of his Sevillian home, where a life less sombre than that of the family brothel was shared with him by his sisters Andrea and Magdalena, and by his brothers Juan, the youngest of them all, and Rodrigo, who was later to be Miguel's companion in misfortune.

All these far-off images passed as though they were present before his half-closed eyes. . . .

Perhaps he remembered, too, the time he had spent in the class-room of that good humanist, López de Hoyos, who nurtured his taste for letters and praised his earliest efforts. Perhaps he remembered the fond farewell of his parents, and his brothers and sisters, when he set out for Italy in Acuaviva's train. . . .

And now what path was he to follow—now that he was all by himself, with nothing on which to rely but his own resources, with nothing to guide him but that not very precise desire of his: that desire of his sketched in roseate scrawls against a dark background, like the clouds which veiled the sun setting over the Roman Campagna?

In one of his pockets he might have a few lines of rhyme; but such things were merely the pastime of people who had no material cares. . . . How was he going to earn his living?

SUPPOSED PORTRAIT OF CERVANTES BY HIMSELF

Perhaps, some time or other, he had heard, from lips dear to him, a story of past greatness, made all the more splendid by remoteness, which went so far as to merge the now humble path of his genealogy in the royal road of the Kings of Galicia.

But Miguel knew that such memories were not coin of the realm. However authentic they might be, if they were to ring true in other people's ears, if they were to be accepted, they must display themselves in the light of glory newly won, or else in the company of any number of yellow *soles*, proclaiming excellence of lineage and condition in golden voices from the depths of purses. . . .

What path was he to follow?

In this deserted garden, stretching itself lazily under the setting sun amid the ruins, there was a lulling silence. When the sun finally disappeared, doubtless even those very thoughts of his, which darted back and forth behind his brow, answering the shrill calls of the swifts in a minor key, would be hushed to silence too.

But suddenly, from the other side of the hill, came a plaintive song, whose words were dulled by distance. He could not tell what the song was all about; but its caressing rhythm enveloped his heart in a soft tenderness, and, though its words did not reach him, words of his own rose to his lips, improvised to match the lullaby of the distant song, and to match his own very close hopes and fears. . . .

It was then, perhaps, that was born that bitter couplet which he was later to put into the mouth of a little squire following the good knight along the roads of Castile :

> " I go to the wars because I must.
> If I had any money, I wouldn't go trussed."

CHAPTER II

Now that impoverished gentleman, Miguel de Cervantes, went clad in the vivid colours that earned the Spanish foot-soldier the nickname of " rooster." He lounged about the streets of Rome and of Naples, leading the leisurely life of men-at-arms in time of peace.

They talked about the news that came from the Christian princes, and from the lands subject to the Turks. It was said that Pope Pius V was making himself the echo of the Venetians, so as to swell their signal of alarm and carry it to the ears of all the princes of Christendom; and that Philip II of Spain—that stout pillar surmounted by the image of the Faith, sole sure supporter of the orthodox and terror of all heretics—was about to hearken to the voice of the Pontiff and put an end to the excesses of the Turkish ships.

Miguel belonged to the company of the captain whom he was himself to dub " famous " in the most famous of all books, Don Diego de Urbina, and to the *tercio* of Moncada. He gained acquaintance with the well-trodden path of the soldier by land and sea, " the authority of quartermasters, the free-and-easiness of some captains, the importunity of billeters, the industry and close reckoning of paymasters, the complaints of the populace, the trafficking in warrants, the insolence of recruits, the argumentativeness of inn-keepers, the overweening demands of porters," and " those sea-port houses where most of the time bed-bugs torment you, criminals rob you, sailors bore you, rats nibble at you, and the sound of the waves wearies you."

Finally Captain Urbina received orders to embark his men aboard the ships of the Marquis of Santa Cruz and proceed, together with other Pontifical and Venetian vessels, to the help of the unhappy Cypriots, threatened by the forces of Selim, son of Soleiman the Magnificent. At Otranto the Spanish galleys kept rendezvous with the Venetian ships of Marco Antonio Colonna and the Pontifical fleet under Giovanni Andreas Doria.

But everybody suffered from thirst to command. The pricks of jealousy hurt them more than the deeper wounds of sword and lance; and what they feared most was not death, which makes all men equal, but lest their own names should fall into that equality on the same level as other people's names.

They could not agree. There was mutual disobedience, mutual recrimination, among Doria, Colonna, and Santa Cruz. It was Mustapha and Ali Pasha who came to an understanding first; and they stormed the capital of Cyprus, unfortunate Nicosia, bearing death, destruction and servitude with them in the swirl of their cloaks, on the edge of their scimitars, in the roll of their kettle-drums.

Perhaps, from the forepeak of his galley, Miguel scanned the horizon where the waves were reddened by the flames, and wept for lost Nicosia in the very words of his *Liberal Lover*:

" Alas, sad ruins of unhappy Nicosia. . . . Alas, ye tumbled towers ! . . ."

In the fertile soil of his imagination, confronted with the pettiness of human pride, flaunting itself as though in a pawnbroker's shop-front, this event sowed the seed which was later to germinate in sublime irony. A gentleman

19

impoverished, but rich in ideas, he felt himself superior to the great ones of the world, whose ideal was a poor little thing, caught in the trap formed by the letters of a name.

After this frustrate expedition, Cervantes went back again to his vagrant life around the ports of Italy, picking up all the wheezes and wangles of veteran soldiers; or else dreaming, with his belly to the sun, on the bluffs above the coast, facing that Latin Sea with its blue slashed by the white of sails.

A love affair, plucked in the facile Italian garden, seems to have borne him up in his hopes, now more impatient than ever for some new, some luckier adventure which would at last open the gates of a different way of life for him. In the autumn of his years, he looked back with such longing upon this vale of his sojourn in Italy, that we must needs suppose that it flowered in a woman's smile.

In the spring of 1571, news came that the Holy League had been reconstituted, and that His Serene Highness Don John of Austria, illegitimate son of the late Emperor Charles V, had been appointed to the supreme command of the allied fleet. In July, Don John sailed from the port of Barcelona with seven-and-thirty galleys. From Genoa, where he was received with triumphal pageants and torch-light processions, he sent summons to Rome and to the Seignury of Venice; and at the beginning of August he called at Naples, on his way to Messina, where he arrived on the 25th.

Miguel embarked at Naples aboard the galley *Marquesa*, commanded by Francisco de San Pedro. His disorderly soldier's life, his frequenting of unhealthy localities, and the preying on his nerves of something indefinite, but something as near at hand as it was grandiose, had left him drawn and feverish.

From his ship he could hear the sounds of the festivities with which Messina welcomed the fleet of the liberators. The plaintive strains of flageolet and rebec, the thundering of mortars firing salutes, the hurrahs of the excited populace, made up a flame in which his impatience grew white-hot. On deck in the moonlight, he trembled with fever and enthusiasm, with his burning eyes staring into the darkness.

Out of all his life, perhaps this was the sole moment—this prelude, this preparation for battle at sea—when a flash of really warlike spirit flickered across his mind. He was far from the born soldier with whom some of his biographers would like to present us.

What attracted him was beauty; and in those days of steel, when, after a ceaseless struggle, her diverse kingdoms had at last come together to make one Spain, powerful and feared, beauty was still to be found in killing and destroying.

As yet Miguel knew nothing about war, unless it were through the medium of epic poems and pompous prose which embellished it with their rhythm and their rhetoric. From the sole occasion when he had come into more or less close contact with it, a few months earlier, at the time of the fall of Nicosia, his warm heart had kept alive only a bloodthirsty desire for revenge upon those who had stormed the city and brought terror and death to its inhabitants.

Later, when the cold of many winters had diminished the enthusiasm of his younger years, when he was old and unfortunate, and, because he was old and unfortunate, humane and understanding, he was to raise the loftiest monument of merriment upon the pedestal of warlike deeds.

It could have been no bellicose spirit who wrought, so lovingly, the figure of the knight who was always beaten, always a butt of derision. But, at that time, the fever of malaria and of enthusiasm not yet spent fired his heart and his mind's eyes.

On 16th September the fleet sailed from Messina. More than three hundred ships rowed out of the port, cleaving the waters of the Inner Sea with the rhythmic strokes of their innumerable oars.

Then on the horizon, away towards where the sun rose, emerged the coasts famed in story and song, circled with a shining halo which linked together thoughts of the past and thoughts of the present. Immortal Greece stretched out her arms to her Latin sons, summoning them to protect her against the attacks of her eternal enemies, come from the cities of the distant Orient. Corfu and Gumeniza watched them pass and sail away towards the port of Cephalonia, where they arrived on 5th October.

Here more sorrowful news awaited them about the destruction, devastation and despair which the Turks were sowing along their path. Mustapha had captured Famagusta and, false to his word, had taken lives and property. He had put the Venetian Bragadino, who commanded the fortress, to death after terrible torture. The poor flayed skin of the vanquished commander streamed in the wind from the mast of the Turkish flagship, a pitiful sight to see.

The very sea rose in revulsion and carried the news on its waves to the Christian ships. The very stars in the sky

22

almost trembled too when the fleet left the shelter of port and sailed north-east, towards the coast of Albania.

Leaning on the bulwarks of the galley *Marquesa*, to cool his fevered brow with the morning breeze, Miguel watched the first light of dawn scatter sparkling gems in the troughs of the sea. The sky veiled its clear, crystalline blue in rosy crape.

Beside him, in a voice choked by anxiety over the coming hours, somebody murmured:

" God keep us all this seventh day of October, in this year of His grace 1571! "

CHAPTER III

WHEN the first shots were fired and trumpets and kettle-drums summoned the fighting-men on deck, Miguel was lying in his bunk, with a high fever setting the blood throbbing at his temples and peopling his brain with fantasies.

At first he scarcely understood what was the meaning of this summons to the jaws of death, this wild shouting of a multitude of men. But he dragged himself to his feet and went on deck again.

Before his eyes was a semi-circle of Venetian galleys, with the standard of the Seignury waving amid clouds of smoke. Further away could be made out the frigates, bergantines and galleys of the Turkish fleet, flaming with the fire of their own cannon, and, in the case of some ships, with the fire which they had received.

A fast ship, flying the commander-in-chief's flag, darted amid the Christian fleet, a restless pedestal for His Serene Highness Don John, whereon he stood like a living statue. In one hand he grasped the standard of the League. He spurred his men into the fray with promises of glory, earthly and heavenly, for every man who bore himself well, and with curt reminders of the enemy's recent misdeeds, which set all hearts thirsting for revenge.

Captain Francisco de San Pedro came up to this soldier of his, whose wan face and tottering legs did not promise that much aid was to be expected from him. The captain suggested that Cervantes should go back to his berth. But

24

Miguel was of no mind to let it be suspected that his feverish trembling was due to fear. With his face flushed for a moment by the flame of his pride, he replied to his captain:

"I have always served His Majesty to the best of my endeavour, and so I shall do now, weak and feverish though I may be. I would rather not go below. I will fight in the service of God and His Majesty, and die for them if need be."

From the neighbouring ships came groans of agony, curses, prayers, the thunder of cannon and musketry, shouts of victory and death-cries. One ship already bore the bleeding trophy of a conquered enemy. The head of Ali Pasha, stuck on a pike, responded grimly to the mute cries for vengeance which, some days before, the heads of the Cypriotes stuck on the Turkish captain's foremast had uttered to the wind and the waves.

The life of Barbarigo, the Venetian admiral, was already ebbing away in a torrent through a mortal wound in his eye; but, with his sight blinded by clouds of blood, he still kept on encouraging his men with voice and gesture. The Viceroy of Alexandria had lost his life, and, with it, the liberty of his men; and the banner that, a few moments earlier, had waved aboard his ship, lashing at the wind as though to punish it for its fickle shifting, which upset his plans and his array, now lay low, in the power of the "Nazarenes."

In his every word, in his whole attitude, Don John was true to the role of exterminating Angel, sent from Heaven, which he played so well; and all was bellowing of wind and sea, roaring of cannon, shouting of Furies unleashed in men's hearts. There was no horizon in the distance, there was no horizon to men's thoughts; for the one was veiled by the smoke of gunpowder, and the other by blood-lust or by fear. There was no Heaven above or in men's souls.

Cervantes fought at the head of a handful of men with whose command the captain had entrusted him; for, simple soldier though he might be, the captain could see in his shining eyes a reflection not so much of fever as of wide-awake wits. The *Marquesa's* skiff was put to sea, and he adventured in her with his harquebusiers.

He brandished his sword towards the foe, careless of his own life, while, before his eyes, ships went down and rent timbers and shattered corpses soared upwards in brief flight. But Heaven, covering its blue eyes with its hands of mist lest it should see the horror of the battle, rejected them, and men and sail sank back into the depths. The ships that remained afloat were dyed dark red, as though they were draping themselves in royal robes to present themselves before the astonished eyes of the people who were later to look upon them.

Captain San Pedro had fallen by now. The handful of men who sailed in the skiff with Cervantes was still smaller after an hour's fighting. Many a young man, ripe fruit proudly flaunted by the tree of life, was stricken down by the hail of lead. But, bowed though he might be beneath the storm, with two harquesbus wounds in his body and one in his left hand, Miguel de Cervantes still stood firm-footed against the hurricane that scattered death.

Even now he could feel that this was an event which would know no equal, a theme for songs, something to be treasured in books and in men's memories for centuries. He could not tell that some poet, ranked as divine in his time

and forgotten today, was to blaspheme the gentle, pitiful
God of Golgotha in his lines:

> " Now Thy day is come,
> Lord of the mighty host."

But he could guess that he found himself present " at the
highest occasion that the centuries have seen," and he
wanted to be a letter in the immortal page which History
was now writing. He did not know that he was himself
to live to write pages bathed in such soft clarity, like moonlight, that all other lights would shrink away and hide for
fear of comparison. What kept him up, in his blood-stained
boat, was neither lust for killing, nor contempt for death,
but his pride in making a good showing, spurred on by his
fever.

But his strength ebbed away through his body wounds,
and his hurt hand hung limp and useless at his left side.
What he saw swam into the visions with which his pounding
blood peopled his brain. All was confusion before him, but
all was confusion also within him, and his eyes refused to
go on seeing, as though they had had enough of such horrors,
and his legs gave way under him.

But, over and above all the din, over and above the
painful buzzing between his temples, rose a shout so loud
that it rent the mist and left clear above his eyes, for a
moment, the pale, transparent blue of twilight:

" Victory for the Christians!"

CHAPTER IV

THE caress of the autumnal sun was soft and soothing when, in the middle of the morning, Miguel left his bunk. Holding on to the handrails of the companion-ways, leaning on a comrade's arm, he made his way on deck to feel the sun's kisses on his maltreated flesh.

His badly bandaged wounds were still bleeding, and his left hand, lost to all sense of obedience, lay listless on his knees and made no effort to second his right hand.

As the ship sailed westward, islands and promontories of the mainland kept on appearing, one after the other, on the port bow, with their olive groves and laurel shrubberies sloping gently down to the sea and murmuring, as the breeze in their leaves gave them voice, about better times, when the world was young.

Miguel forgot his sufferings as he recalled that world no longer to be seen, and he drowsed, lulled by the rocking motion of the waves and the kisses of the sun. All the lovely company of Hellenic nymphs paraded past his half-closed eyes, pursued by Pan, misshapen, bearded, and lustful; and the panoplied procession of heroes who made fine speeches at solemn moments and knew how to die like men.

But some days of the passage were rough. The ships danced on the crested waves, and Miguel feared to find his floating fortress captured by the sea's assault and sunk.

His wounds were already beginning to heal—thanks more to the fewness of his years than to the scanty science of the doctors and surgeons—when they reached Messina on their

28

return from Lepanto. It was the thirty-first day of the same month of October.

The city received the victors with rejoicing, with streets beflagged and triumphal pageants to match those with which it had bidden them Godspeed. As soon as the sails were sighted on the horizon the town was bedecked, and thousands of hands were outstretched towards that constellation of canvas which made its appearance low down in the east, lit by the light of hope. It was as though the city itself opened its arms towards those who brought it the blessing of peace, with nothing more now to be feared.

Already the power of the Turks seemed annihilated for ever. One further slight effort, and all the vast empire which had been built up within so few years, but at the price of such widespread ruin, would draw its elastic, viscous body back into its Asiatic shell.

But the hand that should have launched the final spear against the Crescent—which at this moment, contrary to its symbolism, was waning—hid itself distrustfully beneath its black cloak, for fear of being lopped off. Philip II, that lightning of the Church, would have liked to make an end of his enemy; but his fear was greater than his desire, and he was jealous lest there should grow up in his kingdom, suckled in glory, an eaglet who, if he spread his wings in full flight, might hide from Philip himself the light of that sun which never set on his States. So Don John of Austria was left to parade through all the ports of Italy his triumph, his impatience, and finally his despair.

Venice, too, that city of merchants, thought more of her material interests than of her good name and fame. She sought a truce. She was ready to compromise with those who attacked her cities overseas and flaunted the bloody remains of Venetian captains as trophies of their winning.

A slight effort would have sufficed; but jealousy and greed made such inroads in men's hearts, that even this slight effort proved too much for them. So the Turks were able to recover themselves and renew their preparations, and the opportunity was lost—not to return until four centuries had passed.

Meanwhile Cervantes was convalescing from his wounds in hospital at Messina. All the end of this year and the early months of the next year he spent wondering which he had to worry about most—whether his left hand was permanently crippled, or whether he would ever get rid of his fever.

But in April the days became brighter, and the sun served him as a better doctor than the fumblers of the royal fleet, among whom was to be found no less a light of learning than that distinguished physician Don Gregorio López, who had laid his hands on the august person of the Emperor Charles V.

The three escudos a month whereby Miguel's pay had been increased by His Serene Highness the Admiral Don John; the grants which, as a result of this high recommendation, came into Cervantes' hands—twenty ducats on 15th February, the same amount a week afterwards, and twenty-two ducats more a little later—and divers other sums by way of expenses, costs of his treatment, and recompense of his gallantry: all this, with the aid of the spring, helped to attune his mind in keeping with his years, and turn it away from the shadows of battle and fever, now far behind it.

The Sicilian countryside, the flower-garden of Italy, was a panacea for all his ills too, with its terraced vine-yards covered with fresh green in these April days, its symbolical laurels, and its lime-trees with their verdure of a perennial springtide.

Here, if he had not already done so on the banks of the Guadalquivir at Cordova and Seville, he learnt how to appreciate the charm of life in the country, remote from any jarring note, using all his five senses to taste the delights which were offered to him by the clear water of running brooks, as pleasant to the palate as to the ear, and by the fruits, still unripe, which were all the more tempting for being so near to plucking: just like the passionate glance of puberty's eyes.

All this sensuousness was later to overflow in those pages of his which are closest to reality, the pages of his *Galatea*; and the meadows which he describes as being watered by the fitful flow of the Henares belong rather to his memory than to the real meadows of the Alcarria.

His well-filled leisure created for him a mirage of remoteness into which his present life fitted. It seemed to him now that this soldier's life of his was what suited him best, and he let himself be carried away by the smoothly flowing stream of hours that were all alike. The tastes which had earlier appealed to him most strongly now lay dormant within him, lulled by scented breezes and the songs of brooks and young throats.

He laid aside the pen which he had already launched in soaring flight into the blue empyrean, and his hand that drove it rested from an activity which would have made its labour twofold; for he had to help his mistress and her family with their work, and he felt that this left him no time for intellectual pursuits.

No longer did he people the horizon, as he had once done, with figures impalpable and fantastic. Instead it was pleasantly bounded for him by sweet-smelling orchards. During these brief days of his convalescence, and, soon afterwards, during the scarcely longer ones of his stay in Sardinia, he revelled in all the material blessings that God put within reach of his hand, as though he guessed that later the Creator would be so sparing of His gifts that he would only be able to enjoy the fruits which he found in the fertile garden of his own mind.

But the spring days ended for him sooner than they did for the fields of Sicily. Before May had come, his health was restored, and force of circumstances took him back to the normal routine of a soldier's life.

Now he was in Don Lope de Figueroa's *tercio*, and in Don Manuel Ponce de León's company. But in none of his later writings do we find any enthusiasm for his return to activity; whereas, in some of them, we can feel his fondness for the gentle chains which bound him to his leisurely life in the Latin gardens.

Years later, during the days of his captivity, he wrote to Mateo Vázquez, Philip II's secretary, a rhymed letter in which, after a glowing eulogy of the heroic deeds of Lepanto, bitterness drew from him this confession of his regret that, after his first misfortune in that battle, he had not at once abandoned the career of arms:

> " I sailed the next year's dawning,
> Though mine own mind gave me warning
> That I should rue my scorning."

The ships of the League cruised about the Mediterranean dispersed and at random. The Venetian were separate from the Pontifical, and the Spanish separate from both. Don John waited at Corfu for the allies to renounce their individual expeditions against the Turks. Only late in September did the fruitless enterprise of 1572 begin, with the sailing from the Greek port of the two hundred and eighty ships which made up the fleet of the League.

The Turks, not yet recovered from their defeat at Lepanto, fled before the array of the Christian galleys as they displayed their white winged silhouettes against the blue of sunset. Navarino and Modon were the refuges of the Mussulman ships, and between the two ports Don John extended his squadrons to keep the unity of the enemy fleet broken. But the two parts of the Turkish fleet nevertheless succeeded in uniting, thanks to skilful manœuvring; and Modon was impregnable, if not in the eyes of the Spanish infantry, at least in the judgment of the allied generals, who agreed on withdrawal without attempting an attack. The chance was lost at Navarino, discretion prevailed at Modon, and the whole white array of sail turned back once more towards the West.

"I found myself the next year, which was that of '72, at Navarino, rowing in the admiral's galley with its three lanterns. I saw and noted the opportunity which was there lost of taking the whole Turkish fleet in port, for all the Levantines and Janissaries aboard it regarded it as certain that they would be attacked in the port itself, and they had their clothes and their *pasamaques*, that is to say their shoes, all ready to flee on shore, without waiting to be attacked, such was the fear which our armada inspired.

"But Heaven willed otherwise. . . . In the end, Uchali concentrated at Modon, which is an island not far from Navarino, and, putting his men on shore, blockaded himself at the mouth of the port ; and there he stayed until the Lord Don John retired."

In these frank words Cervantes makes his " captive," the Leonese captain, speak in the famous inn. Miguel, of course, was not himself the rower in the " admiral's galley with its three lanterns," but from the bulwarks of the Christian fleet he stored in his mind what was later to form the subject of bitter accusation by his pen, now wielded by a hand weakened by years and hardship.

Then the " captive " goes on, relating adventures which are not so much his as those of the man who invented him in his own image and likeness :

" In the course of this voyage was taken the galley known as the *Prize*, whose captain was a son of the famous corsair Barbarossa. She was taken by the Neapolitan flagship called the *Wolf*, commanded by that lightning-flash of war, that father of his soldiers, that gallant and never-beaten captain Don Alvaro de Bazán, Marquis of Santa Cruz.

" I must not fail to tell you what happened on the taking of the *Prize*. Barbarossa's son was so cruel and treated his prisoners so badly that, when the rowers saw that the galley *Wolf* was going to ram them, all of them rose up together and seized their captain, who was on the gang-plank shouting at them to row faster ; and, passing him from bench to bench, from stern to bow, they gave him so many buffets that, before he was much further forward than the mast, his soul had already gone to Hell ; such were, as I have said, the cruelty with which he treated them, and the hatred which they had for him."

The whole array of sail, rowers, soldiers and armament, which Christendom had at its disposal to annihilate the already diminished might of the Ottoman Empire, yielded as its sole result the taking of one ship. Still the lyres which were all strung for new songs of heroism could not resign themselves to silence, and Fray Pedro Padilla launched on the wind the strains of his ballad: " When Don John with his armada was at Navarino. . . ."

With the return of the Spanish fleet to Messina and Naples, the campaign of that year came to an end. Cervantes remained in garrison in Naples, and during the winter he may have spent some time in barracks in Sicily.

Once more he had leisure, but now it was unaccompanied by those " aids towards expenses " which last year had proved a pleasant prop for his convalescence. Out of his soldier's pay, increased by three escudos, he had to find himself clothing and food.

But the times were free and easy, and credit was liberal. When the occasion required, or he felt so inclined, he could still find in his purse the few maravedies which a glass of good wine cost—luckier in this than Master de Berceo, who had to beg for it in couplets; or enough to purchase a trinket dear to eyes which looked at him sweetly—happier in this, too, than those lean poets born on the soil of Italy, who never knew what passionate kisses meant.

At the beginning of the year 1573, the intention of the Venetians to come to terms with the Turks became apparent, and Don John had to carry on his enterprises with no other aid than that of God. His knowledge that he was lauded by millions of tongues as a hero, and feared by countless numbers, inspired him with ambition for higher honours. He contemplated making himself master of one of the African kingdoms subject to the Crescent and wearing its crown himself.

But the main resistance to this project of his was forth-

35

coming, not from Aluch Ali—that Uchali of whom the
" captive " speaks—but from the lord of the Spains, Philip
II, suspicious of any greatness which did not belong to his
own person. Don John's project was reduced, by order of
Madrid, to a mere change of crowns, and it was not his
brow which was to be adorned with the spoils of conquest,
but that of Muley Mahomet, who was thought to be
readier than Uchali to bend his neck to the yoke of the
Spanish Court and submit to its wishes.

In September of 1573 Don John's armada sailed from the
ports of Messina and Palermo. Miguel was still in Figueroa's
tercio, and under that leader he took part in the capture
of Tunis.

On the eighth day of October—the day after the second
anniversary of Lepanto—the ships arrived off the port. A
Christian garrison, a legacy of the expeditions of the Emperor
Charles V, still held the fort of La Goulette, opposite Tunis,
and the fort's cannon replied with peaceful salvoes to the
salutes of the ships. No resistance from the discouraged
defenders of the city was encountered, and the Spanish
infantry marched through the Moorish streets to the
rhythmic strains of kettle-drums and flageolets.

But for Cervantes the walls and forts, with which modern
Tunis was surrounded, held less interest than its records of
bygone ages, whose reality comes down to us, through the
lapse of time, coloured with poetry, just as a ray of the sun
assumes all the colours of the iris when it passes through a
polychrome window.

Here was the city founded by Dido and destroyed by
Scipio. Miguel roamed amid the mutilated remains of
Carthage the magnificent. The shade of Æneas came to

meet him in some leafy grove, and, in his company, Cervantes lamented, in Virgil's sweet words, the sad end of the passionate Queen.

After spending a few days in Tunis, settling the question of its sovereignty in accordance with the orders of Madrid, and strengthening the citadel, Don John returned to the ports of Sicily, and Miguel went back with all the other members of the expedition. He wore his soldier's uniform for a few months longer, but his life on active service came to an end with this expedition to Tunis.

So, when the " captive " speaks in melancholy terms of the disastrous end of the defenders of the fort of La Goulette and the city of Tunis, it is on the basis of what came to Miguel's ears from those who were later his companions in misfortune in the prisons of Algiers.

"La Goulette, hitherto regarded as impregnable, was the first to be lost, and it was not lost through any fault of its defenders, who did everything that they should and could have done in its defence. . . . Don Pedro Portocarrero, the commander of La Goulette, who had done everything possible to defend his fortress, was taken prisoner; and he felt his loss of it so much that he died of chagrin on the way to Constantinople. . . ."

In the " captive's " words there breathes a sigh for the fallen; but, in between two pitying paragraphs, the voice of the man of genius raises itself prophetically—for this seems to have been written rather about what was later to happen than about what had already happened:

"But it appeared to many, and so it appeared to me, that it was a particular grace and favour that Heaven bestowed on Spain when it permitted the destruction of that breeding-ground and shelter for knaves, *that sponge, that spendthrift, that waster of the infinity of money that was recklessly spent there,* to no other purpose than that of preserving the memory that it was the luckiest capture of the invincible Charles V. . . ."

Those who tell us about Cervantes' vocation for the career of arms, and the zest with which he embraced it, have not meditated much upon this blunt accusation of his against the " breeding-ground and shelter for knaves." It shows us in how little esteem he held a certain class of men of war, and how utterly lacking he was in enthusiasm for the glorious memories kept alive with the money of the exhausted Spanish treasury.

CHAPTER V

A SHORT stay in Sardinia, after the expedition to Tunis, and a year in Naples, idle and ill-paid, tore out of the calendar of his life, leaf by leaf, the closing days of 1573, the whole of the year 1574, and half the next year.

Of Naples he kept a happy memory which sweetened the sad hours of his later years. There was a love affair whose delights he tasted during these days, but Fate parted the fruit of it from his longing eyes.

With a tenderness unequalled in all the rest of the poem, he speaks to us, at the end of his *Journey to Parnassus*, about that son whom it was given him to embrace only in his dreams. He would have liked to embrace him too, and not merely in imagination, at the end of the long and painful journey of his life.

> " My friend embraced me fondly;
> And, as he held me in his arms, he said
> To find me ever there he had much doubted.
> He called me father, and I called him son.
> With that the truth was out,
> And here I set it down.
> ' In earlier, happier days, my son,' I said,
> ' Here dwelt I in this land,
> When I was young and lusty.' "

Naples peopled his memory with images beloved and lost, perhaps for ever. From the dungeons of Algiers in which he spent years of his youth; from amid the files of his tax-gatherer's office; from behind the bars of the Sevillian prison where he—and his genius—grew to maturity; in the silence of his house in Madrid, where we barely hear a slight rustle of skirts and a stifled sigh, and where, with his sad load of pain and privation, he spent his old age, he turned his eyes towards the smiling shores of "*mare nostrum*," because *there* the continuance of himself survived, the memory of his brightest days made flesh, that son of his whom the provincial lady who united her life to his, with little affection and less desire, had failed to give him. . . . How his hand must have trembled when he wrote those two lines:

> " He called me father, and I called him son.
> With that the truth was out. . . ."

His brother Rodrigo had come to share his soldier's lot. With him, Miguel roamed the streets of Naples, watched the arrival and departure of the galleons of Spain, and picked up from the latest arrivals the news which they brought from Castile, Burgundy and the Indies.

It may be that they led dissolute lives, doing no good to their bodies or their consciences, as Miguel de Castro assures us was the custom among the soldiers of that time. One day they would kick their heels in the ante-rooms of the Cardinal-Viceroy Granvela, waiting to solicit favours or advances on pay that was due to them. Another day they might see, passing through those same ante-rooms, the vindictive Bishop-Inquisitor Don Diego de Simancas, who took the Cardinal's place as Viceroy when Granvela went to Rome to attend a Consistory, and who was himself the prosecutor, before the Pontifical Court, of the unfortunate Archbishop of Toledo, Don Bartolomé de Carranza, accused of heresy on the ground of subtle and incomprehensible strayings from strict orthodoxy.

They talked about everything where soldiers gathered: war, amorous intrigues, exchanges of blows unsanctioned by military authority and even frowned upon by it, envy and jealousy between the rulers of nations and the rulers of consciences. Among all the talkers, none was listened to with greater interest than Cervantes, for he had a pretty wit and an elegant turn of words, he had been singled out for his bravery in the greatest of battles, and he was a distant relation of the magnificent Archbishop of Salerno, Cardinal Cervantes.

But, in the end, the scant respect that was paid to his claims, the irregular life that was corrupting his young body and his freshness of mind, and the hope of better success in the capital, moved Miguel to leave the narrow streets of Naples for the wide highways of the sea.

He had a letter of recommendation from the Duke of Sesa, who had succeeded Lope de Figueroa in the command of his *tercio* and Granvela in the viceroyship of Naples. But what, above all, led him to look upon the future with high hopes was a letter from His Serene Highness Don John, in which he commended the person of the gallant Miguel to his lord and brother Philip as highly deserving to be entrusted with the command of a company.

On 20th September 1575, three galleys sailed from the port of Naples, the *Sol*, the *Mendoza*, and the *Higuera*, all belonging to the squadron commanded by Don Sancho de Leiva. Aboard the *Sol* were Miguel and Rodrigo de Cervantes.

The weather was fine, and their thoughts were attuned to it. Overseas were the shores and the cities of Spain, and, at a street-corner in the capital, a modest house, a haven of hearts already rejoicing over the news of their arrival: their parents and their sisters Magdalena and Andrea. Magdalena now lived in seclusion and wept over her crossing in love; whereas sister Andrea managed to get something more substantial than sobs and sighs out of her disappointments. At this time she was receiving sumptuous presents from the Italian Leocadelo. He was soon to marry somebody else, and then she was to take proceedings against her earlier love, Don Pedro Portocarrero.

The letters which Miguel carried with him, well concealed in his clothes, were a sure token of his future prosperity. If the career of arms was not the one that best suited his tastes and feelings, he knew that we cannot ask of life that it should lead us by the hand along the paths which we like best, but simply, at the most, that it should open a path for us along which we can march without too much trouble.

Everything was attuned to make his thoughts happy ones; the weather, and these high hopes of his. Only the sight of the coasts of Italy, which had disappeared behind him and were now no more than a haze on the horizon, lingered as a vision before his eyes when he turned them away, wrapped his thoughts in a mist of receding images and made them melancholy. He was tempted to feel as though these clouds of melancholy were dissolving into a fine rain of nostalgia upon his heart; but he expected that he would soon come back, and

42

this sufficed to turn his mind away from brooding over sad ideas.

He did not think of saying good-bye to the Latin cities where he had spent the best of his days; for, in that letter of recommendation from Don John, it was suggested that he should command one of the companies destined for Italy. He did not take any farewell of his youth, which he could now feel pounding within him in waves of good health. . . . But, on the horizon, sails appeared.

The three Spanish galleys were coasting along the western shores of Italy towards the Gulf of Lyons. Miguel thought about his loves of Naples, and his more chaste affections in Spain.

Some day, when he had refreshed himself with the sweetness of Spain again, he would return to taste the delights of Italy once more. Once more his eyes would be dazzled by the magnificence of Gaeta, " the strong," of Venice, " the admiration of the ancient world," of Genoa and of Rome. Once more he would know " the frolic of Palermo, the plenteousness of Milan, the feasting of Lombardy "; and all of them with the same youthful zest of his twenty-eight years of to-day. . . .

But, on the horizon, sails appeared.

He was never to go back to Italy again. He was never to find his youth again.

From his humble home in Castile—so he told himself— he would go on remembering, together with his loves and his friends there, all those pleasant places, the bright background of the best years of his life. He would stroke those memories of his, softly, silently.

43

He would put into his caressing of them all that treasure of tenderness which swelled his heart even now, off the Three Marys, that landmark near Marseilles, just when, one autumn day of 1575, sails appeared on the horizon.

CHAPTER VI

THE galliots which were advancing to meet the three Christian ships were also three in number, under the command of the Algerine captain Arnaute Mami. But the *Mendoza* and the *Higuera*, the two ships which had sailed with the *Sol*, were not at the moment in company with her. The galley in which Cervantes sailed had to face the corsair vessels all alone.

Through the mist on the horizon were to be seen the shores of the pleasant land of France, with their slopes covered with pines, their orchards gilded by the autumn, murmuring through the voice of the breeze a tale of bucolic peace, and a life without glory and without surprises.

With Miguel, some renowned captains sailed in the galley, among them Don Pedro Díaz Carrillo de Quesada, sometime governor of the lost La Goulette, and a Knight of Saint John of Jerusalem, Don Juan Bautista Ruiz de Vergara. With eyes sombre but undismayed, they gazed at the enemy who were approaching as fast as press of sail and galley-slaves could carry them.

It was the last hour of the day, and over the sea, where Spain lay, the horizon was lit with red streamers, as though a gust of blood, a gust of sorrow, were rising to meet the Spaniards and bar their way to their homeland.

When night fell, the enemy had come up with them and surrounded them; but the corsairs awaited the light of the new day before attacking. The night was one of anxiety; and the day that dawned one of bitterness.

"The enemy were not slow in coming up with us," Cervantes tells us in his *Galatea*, through the mouth of Timbrio, just as elsewhere he puts real events in his own life into the mouths of his characters,

"and the wind was still less slow in falling, which was the main cause of our perdition. The enemy did not attempt to board us yet, for, seeing that the wind was falling, they thought it better to wait before attacking us.

"This they did, and, when the day came, though we had already counted them, we saw that there were *fifteen* of them" (only in this number, perhaps, does an element of imagination enter into his narrative), "ships of heavy tonnage which had us surrounded, and then the fear that we were lost was confirmed in our hearts. Nevertheless, neither our gallant captain nor any of those who sailed with him was dismayed, and we waited to see what the enemy would do.

"When it was lighter, they lowered a boat from their flagship, and sent it, with a renegade as their spokesman, to summon our captain to surrender, since he must see that it was impossible for him to fight against such a number of ships, more especially as they were the finest ships of Algiers. On behalf of Arnaute Mami, his commander, the renegade threatened that, if our ship fired a single shot, he would hang our captain from the yard-arm when he captured him, adding other threats besides.

"The renegade urged our captain to surrender; but our captain refused to do so, and told the renegade to keep clear of our ship, if he did not want his boat to be sunk by our guns. When Arnaute heard this reply, he commenced to close in on our ship from all directions, discharging his guns as he came with such speed, fury and din that it was a wonder to behold.

"Our ship did the same, and so luckily that one of the ships fighting us ahead went to the bottom; for one of our cannon balls hit her on the waterline, so that within a short time the sea swallowed her up without hope of salvation. When they saw this, the Turks pressed us harder than ever, and in the space of four hours they attacked us four times, and as many times they withdrew with heavy losses on their side and no small ones on ours.

46

" But, lest I should weary you with details of what happened in this battle, I shall simply say that, after we had fought them off for sixteen hours and our captain and most of those aboard our ship had been killed, at the end of fresh attacks on us they finally succeeded in boarding the ship. . . ."

Further on, after relating other incidents which belong rather to fiction than to reality, as the foregoing appears to do, Cervantes adds :

" So, quite unconscious, I was carried aboard the enemy flagship, where they were at some pains to nurse me."

The two Spanish ships which had parted company with the *Sol* now came up, and the corsairs, declining the risk of beginning the battle over again with opponents who were fresh, transferred their prisoners and anything of value in the captured ship to their own vessels, and fled from the scene of their misdeeds, leaving the Christian galley abandoned, red with the blood of its defenders and their enemies.

Among the dead were the captain of the galley and the Knight of Saint John of Jerusalem. Among the prisoners, carried against their will to Algiers, were the brothers Miguel and Rodrigo de Cervantes, both wounded and the worse for wear.

Their new master, the captain of the galliot in which they crossed the Mediterranean, was named Dali Mami. He was a renegade Greek shipmaster, lame, avaricious and cruel.

That letter which bore the signature of Don John of Austria, that letter which Miguel carried sewn into his clothing as his most precious treasure, had been the golden key which was to open the door of the future to him. Now that he was in the power of Dali Mami, it was still a key, but a key to a dungeon. Into a dungeon he was to go, and

47

there his youth was to be wasted; for the avaricious ship-master believed, because of this letter, that he had in his hands one of the most important personages of the kingdom of the Spains, and that his coffers ought to be filled with gold as the price of his prisoner's ransom.

Thus, within the space of a few hours, the whole course of Miguel de Cervantes' life was changed. This was not through the work of chance or of men. It was because Providence elected to mould its chosen vessel between the hands of suffering, so that afterwards, ripe as succulent fruit, it should distil, drop by drop, the sap of its mellow, humane irony.

CHAPTER VII

ONE day at the end of September 1575, three corsair ships were sighted off the port of D'ezair, that city of impregnable defences.

As the silhouettes of the three ships loomed up over the horizon, with sails furled and oars rising and falling, people began to flock to the mole. In guttural, confused murmurs they discussed the possibility of a victory, the name of the captain who might command this squadron. From the whitewashed terraces which descended in an amphitheatre to the port, black eyes scanned the marine expanse through slits in white veils, with lids lowered to protect their pupils against the burning glare of the noonday sun reflected in the sea.

Then the galleys doubled the breakwater of the port and came on, to the accompaniment of the cadenced rhythm of their oars in the water, until they reached the mole. There, no doubt, other corsairs awaited them. They had put money or men into Arnaute Mami's expedition; or else they wanted to see his prisoners and his booty, in case there should be any opportunity for barter of men and merchandise.

Most of them were renegades who desired to make their new brothers in religion forget their origin by excelling themselves in cruelty towards those whom but yesterday they called friends and compatriots. Among them may have been the Genoese Hassan Fornaro, the Greek Caur Ali, the Catalan Mami, or the Murcian Maltrapillo.

Like homing eagles, the pirate bergantines sank their

D

claws into their own nest. The grapples of their anchors plunged into the sea with a croaking of rusty iron. Water splashed over their sides and over the mole, in little drops, pierced by the burning sun, that looked like handfuls of precious stones scattered to the multitude by some prince out of the *Arabian Nights*.

Through the ranks of the onlookers—Bedouin, Arabs, Turks, Jews, renegades, Kabyles and Biskris—the victors made their way, surrounded by a court of welcoming voices, shouts of acclamation, envious looks, bowed heads and bent backs. Arnaute Mami, the commander of the squadron, and the lame Dali Mami, who had stormed the Spanish galleon with the men of his bergantine, swept superbly through the crowd of spectators and vanished into the multitude, on their way to their palaces, where black-eyed Moorish girls awaited them, and fountains which murmured an endless song, monotonous in its rhythm as a song of the desert, under the sweet shade of palms and myrtles.

Behind them came the lamentable procession of the galley-slaves and the new prisoners, some of whom were to take their seats with the galley-slaves,

" shackled to the hard bench of a Moorish galley,"

while others were to await ransom for days and days in the prisons of Algiers.

Among these prisoners marched the captains Díaz Carrillo de Quesada and Ruíz Pérez de Biedma, and the soldiers Juan Valcarcel and Rodrigo de Cervantes. Among them marched, too, another soldier, who had a hand of no use for pulling an oar, and who carried upon his person a letter which lauded his high deserts and bore the signature of the prince Don John of Austria.

His maimed left hand delivered him from the hell of the galleys. But his letter aroused the greed of Dali Mami, who judged him a good capture, worth a high price, and therefore kept him closely and uncomfortably confined, in order to spur his family on with sending his ransom and make sure of the heap of gold that his liberty was surely worth.

The prisoners allotted to Dali Mami made their way up through the steep, twisting lanes of Algiers. They climbed to the palace of the Pasha, where Captain Díaz Carillo, chosen by the viceroy as his share of the booty, was left behind. Then they returned once more to the tortuous narrow streets, in whose walls opened the cramped shops of embroiderers, harness-makers, armourers, and sellers of silks and perfumes brought from the distant East or seized in corsair raids.

Nearly half the day the captives spent in this long following of their path of bitterness. When they reached their lame lord's mansion, they were broken in body and mind, fainting with fatigue and hunger.

Their prison was two floors of galleries opening on to a courtyard, beside Dali Mami's palace. From the hill on which it stood, peeping out over the balcony of the upper gallery, Cervantes could overlook the sea and the white city bathing its feet in the blue waters.

Amid its minarets and its whitewashed flat roofs, rose up the tapering trunks of palms, the solemn silhouettes of cypresses, the graceful, verdant lines of laurels and orange groves. This charming view, as it presented itself for the first time to his eyes, may have made him forget the bitterness of his captivity for a moment; but the limitless sea on the horizon spoke to him of freedom and flight, and the darkness which was falling over the city clutched at his heart with its shadowy claws.

Already the murmur of the streets was dying away, going to ground, hiding itself in mysterious corners where fountains sang and guitars throbbed. Night spread before his eyes over the silenced city, and, within his mind, darkness spread too, over his thoughts, which held no sound of hope.

Suddenly, from all directions, rose a chant slow and somnolent. It ascended in quavering tremolos, scattered and sank, and was answered as though by an echo from minaret to minaret. It rose once more in plaintive trills.

Miguel felt that melancholy melody piercing his heart. He wept his first captive's tears, while the words of the chant seemed to gather together in tenuous clouds under the starry sky:

"There is no God but Allah. . . . There is no help, there is no strength, save in God! . . ."

CHAPTER VIII

AFTER his first dejection, Miguel rose above the pains and sorrows of captivity. His mind, which was later to yield such mature fruit, was now being worked upon by the travail of misfortune; but he kept what it taught him to himself, until it should bring forth fragrant flowers and succulent sap. His spirit soared in daring flights, and looked down from the clouds upon the littleness of all misadventure and of all greatness.

He became the heart and soul of that unfortunate body of slaves. To him came those who sought advice. In him confided those who were not afraid of risking their lives, if adventure held a chance of winning them freedom. From the slave-compound arose a voice calling upon the princes of Christendom, in the measured beat of its hendecasyllables, to turn their eyes towards those who groaned in captivity, to the shame of the peoples who called themselves civilised. In the darkness of Miguel's prison were being born the illuminated pages of his *Galatea*.

Here, in Dali Mami's keeping, he made the acquaintance of Sergeant Navarrete, a dissolute fellow, little minded to go on enduring in patience the privations of captivity; Francisco de Meneses, a young captain who had been taken prisoner at La Goulette; Ensign Rios, the knight Osorio, and the noble Castañeda.

In whispers during their sleepless nights, they plotted together to evade the vigilance of their lame master's myrmidons and make their way to Oran, a port which was in the hands of Spain.

While they awaited an opportunity, Miguel wrote Mateo Vázquez, Philip II's influential secretary, a letter in which he lamented the unhappy lot of himself and his comrades in captivity, and confessed the bitterness of his early days and the despair that had first overwhelmed him:

> " When captive here I came and saw this land,
> So world-wide infamous, which in its breast
> Nurtures so great a pirate brood,
> My will could not my sobs restrain
> And all at once I found my face
> Furrowed by bitter tears."

But Mateo Vázquez, the arch-secretary, as Cabrera de Córdoba calls him, son of the Sevillian canon Don Diego Vázquez Aldarete, was more concerned about not losing the ear of his lord the King than about other people's troubles. When, after long delay, Cervantes' letter came into his hands, the Court was convulsed by the assassination of Escobedo, Don John of Austria's secretary, at the hands of hired bravoes. This was the sequel to a long chain of hatred and perversion of the truth: a chain which ran from the passionate, vengeful heart of the Princess of Eboli to the austere, sombre heart of the King, passing on its way through the Machiavellian heart of Antonio Pérez.

The Princess wanted to satisfy a personal spite against Don John of Austria's secretary. Escobedo had formerly been in the service of the late Prince of Eboli and Duke of Pastrana, and he therefore thought himself entitled to reproach the Prince's widow for her love affair with Antonio

Pérez, another of the King's secretaries. Pérez, egged on by the lady, depicted Escobedo's arrival at the Court to Philip as a manœuvre on the part of Don John of Austria, whom he accused of seeking a crown for himself, to the detriment of the States of his brother and lord. Philip, thus misled, sanctioned Escobedo's assassination.

Antonio Pérez looked upon Mateo Vázquez as his enemy. He feared that Vázquez was on the track of his trickery and his complicity in Escobedo's murder. Vázquez was therefore busy defending himself against Pérez's hatred and intrigues. He was too busy to try to persuade the King to undertake an armed expedition against Algiers in order to free the captive Christians; and so Cervantes' letter to him remained unanswered.

Of no more avail were the letters which Miguel sent to his family—not from any lack of goodwill on their part, but from sheer lack of means. Every one of them did what he or she could to help the two captive brothers; but not all of them together could raise the necessary money. Their father asked for a record of his sons' services, in order to justify him in applying to the royal treasury for the amount of their ransom; their mother petitioned; and one of their sisters pursued her career of amorous adventure, while the other prayed.

Miguel's first attempt at escape must have been made soon after his arrival in Algiers and before he wrote to Mateo Vázquez, for over his letter to Vázquez disappointment flutters like a moth that has singed its wings in trying to approach a light.

> " When these things come back to my mind,
> The tears spring to my eyes. . . ."

Finally Miguel came to an understanding with all his new friends, and they looked round for a guide to show them the way to Oran; seventy leagues across barren, broken country and through bush. Lions still roared in the moonlit nights of Barbary, and snakes lay in wait beside the streams. Nomad tribes which pitched their tents in the eastern plains between Algiers and Oran lived on marauding and hunting down fugitives, whom they handed over to their masters for a handful of money or a firearm. It was too risky to attempt the journey without the escort of somebody familiar with refuges against the attacks of men and wild beasts.

Miguel had come to enjoy comparative liberty. To him resorted all those captives who needed advice and remedies for curing fever, from which he had suffered so much himself that he knew how to combat it. His cultured, attractive manner of speech and his level head endowed him with an authority among the captives which he was far from seeking on his own account. He used it solely for the benefit of those who were suffering. His jailers, and even his lame master himself, treated him with respect. He went from one prison to another.

In the course of these comings and goings of his, he met a Moor who was a muleteer and carrier among the eastern towns. Miguel thought that he had found the man he needed.

In the secret were Captains Francisco de Valencia, Beltrán de Salto, and Ruiz Pérez de Biedma; Ensigns Castañeda and Rios; Sergeants Navarrete and Gómez de Monsálvez, and some others, Hernando de la Vega, Juan de Valcázar, Osorio, and Rodrigo, Miguel's brother—eleven in all, besides Miguel himself.

On the appointed night, eluding the vigilance of their jailers, they assembled at a quiet spot, sheltered under the walls of the city, knocked off the chains which branded them as captives, and made their way along paths which the guide pointed out to them.

In the distance, the sea was peopled with lights, and, when the moon peeped out through a break in the clouds, it bathed in clarity Arnaut Mami's ships, which were just setting out on an expedition in search of booty. On the terraces of Bab el Oued were white shadows whose motionless figures stood out against the darkness of the night, and from the gardens of Algiers came the rustle of leaves and the tinkle of fountains.

All was still in the quiet of night. The very silence spoke to them of other such nights in the gardens of Andalusia or Valencia; but then they had known none of the anxiety that now make them speak and tread softly, lest they should once more awaken misfortune. It seemed to be asleep; but in fact it was still wide awake and lying in wait for them.

At dawn they reached a valley in which there was a spring and a grove of fruit-trees. Here their guide gazed dubiously at the horizon. He said that he had lost his way and must go back on his tracks to find out just where they were. He went off, and he never came back. He had been seized with dread of the punishment that awaited him if Mami the shipmaster ever discovered that he had assisted the escape of his slaves.

They waited for him all day long, but there was no sign of him. Cervantes tried to put fresh heart into his disconsolate comrades and keep their spirits up; but, when night covered the sky once more, it darkened his own thoughts and hopes too.

Nobody among them knew the way to Oran. Despite this, Miguel and Rodrigo were in favour of marching westwards, at random. But the others declared that this meant going to certain death, for hunger, thirst, wild men and wild beasts awaited them.

The next dawn, they set off back to the city. They reached its gates as night was falling, starving and exhausted. Just at the hour when, from the tall minarets, softly floated down the call to faith and hope, they buried themselves once more in their dungeon and their despair.

CHAPTER IX

THE fugitives spent days and days in the dungeon by way of punishment for their attempted escape. When they were let out again, it was to go and work in the quarries and on the fortifications of the port, under the walls of Bab el Oued, which were being repaired at this period.

They were loaded with chains, and they had to work under the African sun—they who probably had never known any greater hardship than that of marching and counter-marching through the valleys of Italy, gay with flowers and fair faces, and across the pleasant plains of Flanders.

Miguel had no greater punishment to bear than that of being appointed overseer of his comrades' punishment. His misfortune, his crippled hand, proved a good fortune in all this sum of adversity.

In the course of this work he made the acquaintance of new comrades in captivity: Don Antonio de Toledo, who, like Don Francisco de Valencia, was a Knight of the Order of Saint John, and of equally high renown for his feats of arms; and Ensign Don Diego de Castellanos, who had been with Miguel in Italy in the days of their free and easy soldiering.

Once more the idea of escape flattered him with its hopes. By chance, he became friends with a slave of the Greek renegade Hassan, governor of Algiers. This slave named Juan, and came from Spanish Navarre. He worked as a gardener on one of his master's estates on the outskirts of the city. He was no less eager to regain his liberty than the other prisoners, and he agreed with them to make a bid for it. As on the first occasion, it was left to Miguel to find the opportunity.

Aid was also offered them by a native of Melilla, who leapt as lightly and sure-footedly from one religion to another as a dog over a Saint John's Night bonfire. He was known as the Gilder, and he had been first a Christian, then a Mussulman, and was now once more a Catholic.

They were busy with the preliminaries of their attempt when some Redemptorist Fathers arrived in Algiers. Among them was Fray Jorge del Olivar, a saint among saints. The Cervantes family, out of their own resources and with some official help, had now scraped together a few doubloons. They were insufficient for Miguel's ransom, because Dali Mami regarded him as an important personage.

Miguel advised his brother to accept liberty for himself alone, if his master, who was now Ramadan Pasha, viceroy of Algiers, would accept the sum sent from Spain. He agreed to accept it, and Rodrigo de Cervantes departed, now with his wrists and ankles freed from fetters, together with another Spanish gentleman, a friend of both of them, one Viana, a Majorcan and, according to Father Haedo, " a man practised in the seas and the coasts of Barbary."

In the leave-taking between the two brothers, the original project of the second attempt at escape was thrown aside. But, when Rodrigo clasped Miguel in his arms in farewell, the loving heart of the brother who stayed behind did not beat more faintly over their separation, and the spectacle of a liberty which he could not himself enjoy. On the contrary, it was borne up by the hope of early release.

Rodrigo and Viana carried letters from the two Knights of Saint John to the viceroys of Valencia, Majorca and Ibiza, recommending them to co-operate in the proposal which Miguel de Cervantes explained to them in a separate letter.

What he proposed was the chartering of a brigantine, which, under the command of Viana, was to approach the Barbary coast on an appointed day to pick up the captives, who would be ready and on the look-out for it.

But there were many slaves who did not know anything about Cervantes' plan. They could not be taken into the secret, for there were thousands of them and the ship could only hold the prearranged number. Among these captives, who had now lost all hope of redemption, there were some whose hearts faltered, whose constancy in resignation wavered. They showed signs of being ready to change their position, since that of a captive was so uncomfortable, turn their backs on their consciences, and pray with their faces towards the East, where lay the tomb of the Prophet.

The saintly Jorge del Olivar—a saint not yet venerated on any altar—came to the aid of the wavering with good words, and to the aid of the weak with still better ones. He offered his own person as a pledge that some day the ransoms which he could not offer at the moment would arrive. So some of the captives were freed, while he remained in the prisons of Algiers, paying for other people's liberty with his own.

He offered his body to the dungeon in an even more sublime sacrifice than that of the martyrs. They died in the hope of a better life, ready to purchase that life of to-morrow for themselves at the price of their sufferings of to-day.

61

Jorge del Olivar suffered in order that the hope of eternal felicity should not be irremediably denied to others.

Meanwhile, those of the captives whose hopes were fixed on Miguel de Cervantes' plan kept on vanishing from the prisons one by one. In Governor Hassan's garden there was a grotto hidden among rosebay and myrtle. The place was pleasant and safe, and Miguel chose it as the rallying-point of the fugitives.

During the day, the shade in the grotto protected these unfortunates from the rays of the summer sun and from inopportune eyes. When the evening breeze came to whisper to them through the orange groves and the myrtle thickets, summoning them to enjoy the garden and its luscious fruits in peace, they left their refuge and, stretched beside a murmuring stream, let their thoughts fly towards the land of Castile, along the shining pathway of Saint James.

Through a sheer miracle of will-power, by dint of resort to all kinds of devices, Miguel in his own penury obtained food for his friends. The Gilder brought it to Hassan's garden, and there the slave Juan hid it away until he found a favourable opportunity for handing it on to the poor men.

So they spent seven anxious months, voyaging in that immovable ship of their hopes which sank, over and over again, into the depths of disappointment. But at last, in the middle of September of this year, which was the year 1577, Miguel received word that Viana's bergantine would soon set sail, and he went and joined his friends in the grotto in the garden.

Governor Hassan's estate was close to the sea. During clear nights, from the gentle slopes of the garden, they could see lights crossing the water and the reflection of the moon which, as it rose in the west, pointed the way to Spain for them with its jewelled forefinger.

One night they heard a muffled sound of approaching oars. Their lips kept silent, because their anxious hearts were in their throats. Their smiles were not to be seen in the darkness, but everybody could guess his comrades' smiles from his own. Groping hands met in clasps of relief and hope. The oars came nearer still, and, mingling with the sound of them, low-voiced orders were to be heard.

But, all at once, these sounds turned into shouts of alarm and sudden scuffling over the waves. Then, once more, there fell silence; silence deep and heart-rending, as though at this moment life had come to an end.

They did not dare to exchange ideas. They kept on listening. Nothing to be heard. . . .

They chose to believe that their hopes had deceived their ears, rather than that freedom had come so close to them and was now withdrawing from almost within their grasp. So they kept on waiting for some sound, watching for some light, to rend the veil of the silence and darkness of this night, blacker than any other night because they could feel its blackness within their own hearts. They kept on waiting. Nothing to be heard. . . .

Miguel ventured down to the beach. His heart was afire. He would have liked to tear it out to illuminate the distant darkness. . . .

When day dawned, disappearing over the horizon was the hull of a Christian ship.

CHAPTER X

" BECAUSE the sailors' hearts failed them, and they dare not leap ashore to give the word to those who lay hidden, our flight was foiled."

So says Miguel de Cervantes, bitterly. But Father Haedo declares, and perhaps he is nearer to the truth, that some Moors happened to pass by, just as the disembarkation was taking place, and gave the alarm, so that there was nothing for the rescuers to do but put to sea again.

When, two days later, the Majorcan frigate tried to get into touch with the shore again, Miguel and his friends were already groaning in the dungeons of the new viceroy of Algiers, Hassan Pasha, that " enemy of all the human race," as Cervantes calls him. The ship fell into an ambuscade, and its crew lost their own liberty—just because their hearts had failed them two days earlier, if Miguel's version of what happened be the right one.

The Gilder, that Melilla Christian who turned apostasy into a regular business, sold his friends as light-heartedly as he was in the habit of selling his gods. On the day which followed their night of anxiety and dying hopes in the garden grotto, he appeared before the viceroy to denounce the fugitives.

Hassan Pasha was covetous, cruel and a pervert. He had been Uchali's favourite, and now he was a lover of gold and of blood. The news which the twofold renegade brought him filled his heart with delight, for it offered him an opportunity both of increasing his wealth and of gloating over the spectacle of other people's sufferings. These slaves who had got so far in their attempt at escape would now belong not to their former masters, but to the viceroy himself. The Gilder was making Hassan Pasha a magnificent present.

Eleven men on horseback and twenty-two on foot set off for the governor's garden. That Judas known as the Gilder guided them.

"When the Turks and the Moors reached the caves and burst into them," writes Miguel in his record of his services,

"Miguel de Cervantes, seeing that they were discovered, told his comrades that they should all throw the blame on him, promising them that he would take it all upon himself, in the hope of saving the rest of them; and so, while the Moors were fettering them, Miguel de Cervantes declared aloud, so that the Turks and the Moors might hear him:

"'None of these Christians who are here has any blame in this matter, for I alone was the author of it and it was I who persuaded them to take to flight.'

"In this, manifestly he was putting himself in danger of death, for the viceroy Azan was so cruel that, just because a Christian tried to escape or because anybody sheltered or aided him in his flight, he would order a man to be hanged, or, for the same crime, have his ears and nose cut off. And when the said Turks sent a man on horseback to inform the viceroy of all that had happened, and of what Miguel de Cervantes said, namely, that he was the author of this hiding and attempted flight, the viceroy commanded that he alone should be brought before him; and the Moors and the Turks brought him fettered hand and foot, loading him with insults and affronts on the way."

His way back to the city was a more painful one than the last time, when his first attempt at escape failed. Now Miguel was taken back by myrmidons who flung taunts

E

65

in his face, and prodded him on like some dangerous beast to make him keep up with their mounts.

He was treated like a criminal; but he had no crime on his conscience, except that his frustrated attempt had compromised his comrades in captivity, who might have to suffer with him for his failure. Perhaps he saw, on the horizon of his thoughts, the sublime smile of the immortal knight, charging lance in rest against all harquebusiers and constables, against all the tyrannies that shackled bodies and minds.

But nobody came to set him free. He could look for no outside aid. Once the grotto hidden in the trees was discovered, he took refuge in that castle of his own greatness of soul, where nobody could reach him.

He was aware of recent cases of flights that failed, and of the torture in which the unfortunate captives who had attempted them had died. There was that of Don Martín de Córdoba who, a few years before, had tried to lead a rising of the Christian captives on behalf of the King of Spain. There was the still more recent one of the two Spanish knights who had suffered execution on the gallows in punishment of their longing for liberty, which they had sought along the road to Oran, the same road which Cervantes himself had followed the first time.

All this Miguel knew. Nevertheless, he had taken the blame of all upon himself, and clasped it to his breast in the hope that punishment would fall upon him alone.

The poor gardener was to be hanged from the highest tree in the garden, tied by one foot, so that he should be choked by his own blood; and Miguel expected no better fate.

But when the viceroy of Algiers, that enemy of the human

race, found himself face to face with a captive looking the worse for being goaded and hustled along; when he expected to see this wretch fall on his knees and beg for mercy, Hassan Pasha was driven instead to look with admiration upon the figure of a man who, with a supreme effort of pride, held himself erect, asked for no clemency, showed no sign of fear or dismay, and did not attempt to unload his faults on other people, but, on the contrary, was ready to take both theirs and his for his own. The viceroy's voice, the taunts that rose to his lips, were stifled in his throat by his astonishment.

Miguel de Cervantes did not suffer the fate that everybody feared for him, and that he had faced without flinching. Hassan Pasha, overcome by the captive's proud bearing, showed himself merciful for once. He bought the prisoner from his master for five hundred gold escudos, and sent him to his own prison.

This lack of severity, this purchase on the part of the viceroy of Algiers, are hard to understand when we have it from his own lips, according to Father Haedo, " *how closely he held the maimed Spaniard guarded, and under what close watch he kept his Christians, his ships, and indeed the whole city, so much did he fear the plots of Miguel de Cervantes.*"

We can only suppose that the despot's clemency was due to an involuntary admiration which kept his blood-stained hands tied. We can only suppose that his purchase of Cervantes from his master was due to his desire to keep Miguel better guarded under his own eyes, and still more to his itch for gold; for he could not imagine that the man who bore himself in such a way was no exalted prince, but simply a poor gentleman.

67

The viceroy had a right, inasmuch as Miguel was a recaptured runaway, to take him from his earlier master for nothing; but Dali Mami was not the man to let himself be despoiled easily. Miguel might be worth a high ransom; and so Hassan Pasha came to terms, which he regarded as on the whole favourable to himself, with the lame pirate. Now the viceroy held Cervantes as his own property, shackled with a chain in the dungeons of his own prison. There Miguel stayed for five months, half-starved and ill clad, wretched and anxious.

From time to time, news came to him how cruelly the viceroy was treating his captives, and this saddened him more than his own sufferings.

"They put a chain on me, rather as a sign that I was held to ransom than to fetter me," he says through the mouth of his " captive,"

"and so I spent my days in that prison, together with many other gentlemen and personages of importance, selected and held to ransom; and, although hunger and cold might sometimes afflict us, and indeed did afflict us almost all the time, nothing afflicted us so much as our hearing and seeing on all sides with what hitherto unknown, with what unheard-of cruelty my master (Hassan Pasha) was treating the Christians. Every day he would hang one of his captives, impale another, cut the ears off a third; and this for such small occasion, or for none at all, that the Turks themselves recognised that he did it just for the pleasure of doing it. . . .

"The only man who fared well with Hassan," this same " captive " goes on,

"was a Spanish soldier named Saavedra, whom, because he had done things that remained in the memory of those people for many years, and all to win his liberty, never did Hassan beat, or order to be beaten, or even speak a harsh word to him; although for the

68

least of the things that he had done we all feared that he would be impaled, and so he feared himself more than once."

This arrogance of the captive became, in the course of his painful days, an armour which masked from the tyrant's eyes the fact that his flesh was as weak as that of any other man. The viceroy of Algiers came to believe that Miguel's body was as indomitable by suffering as his mind. Hassan Pasha gave up trying to subdue it, forgetting that the iron of punishment must make the hands it fettered tremble in the end.

Nor are the pardonable praises of himself which Cervantes sings in connection with that "soldier named Saavedra" mere exaggerations of vanity. Haedo, Archbishop of Palermo, goes beyond them, in his *Martyrs of Algiers*, when he writes:

"Miguel de Cervantes kept their spirits up at the great risk of his life, which he was four times on the point of losing, impaled, hanged or burned alive, on account of what he did to give freedom to many. . . ."

This tribute, it may be added, is not a smoke of incense burned before the image of genius; for, at the time when Haedo wrote it, Miguel de Cervantes Saavedra meant nothing more to the archbishop than "a distinguished gentleman of Alcalá de Henares."

When Miguel was released from his dungeon and allowed to walk in the courtyard, he found relief from his troubles in the pleasant company of some other gentlemen and in writing. Here, no doubt, were born some of those plays of his with an Algerine setting: *The Prisons of Algiers, The Great Sultana Doña Catalina de Oviedo, The Usages of Algiers,* and that delightful story of the "captive" which was later to form a part of the loftiest literary monument that the ages have ever seen.

With his comrades in captivity he talked about their lost homeland, so near at hand in mere distance, but so remote for them. His words wafted them the odour of eastern gardens or northern orchards. Sometimes, when their toil left them a little leisure, and they could forget their troubles for a moment, they composed songs, played charades, or invented games which turned their minds back to the sweet days of childhood.

But few of their hours were so pleasantly spent. Only too many of them pursued the thorny paths of work and want. Only too often they had to leave their holidaying because " they were summoned to the labours that killed them."

The captives of the viceroy of Algiers numbered two thousand. The slave-compound was a dreary place. Its walls, though leprous and tumble-down, were stout enough, and they shut off the horizon. Inside it, the cells were grouped round a courtyard, in whose centre was a water tank. They were dark and badly ventilated. In the air hung a reek of herded humanity, an atmosphere of depression which so many sighs thickened, that it almost seemed to veil that quadrilateral of blue, the luminous canopy of the courtyard. The cell doors closed with a harsh creaking of rusty hinges. By night came the quavering cry of the owls that nested in the ruins and the barking of hungry jackals.

Cervantes could not resign himself to letting his days pass in this misery, without making at least an effort to break his chains, even though he should cripple his hands

70

in the attempt, as had happened to him before. From Spain came consolation and hope, but no certainty of ransom.

His family ransacked their coffers and searched their memories to get together the gold which would free the captive. Their last tapestries and trinkets, their last souvenirs of happier days, went to the pawnbroker in the hope of making up the sum required to end the troubles of their dear son, their dear brother. Doña Magdalena Cervantes, that sweet sister of Miguel's, sued Don Alfonso Pacheco de Portocarrero—but without success—for the sum of five hundred ducats which he had promised her in payment of certain favours. Andrea contributed her last two hundred ducats: doubtless due to the munificence of the Florentine Santes Ambrosio, who about this time, or a little later, became her husband; or perhaps a legacy of her earlier love affair with that other Italian, Leocadelo.

Miguel's disconsolate parents worked tirelessly. They assembled documents, they swore statements, to show the high merits of their son. His praises were sung by all the captives who had already been ransomed and returned from Algiers.

But even all this did not suffice. There were interminable delays. Every effort on Miguel's behalf ran into that bad luck of his which mounted guard over any path that might lead him to good fortune.

Miguel, driven to rely solely on his own wits and resources, made one more attempt at escape.

The fortress of Oran was under the command of Don Martín de Córdoba, Marquis of Cortes, who had himself experienced the bitterness of captivity. Miguel knew this, and it seemed to him a good enough reason why Don

Martín should be ready to help him in his attempt. Accordingly Miguel wrote him a letter asking him to do so. He entrusted it to a poor Moor, whose name is not recorded in any of his writings.

If any reproach can be levelled against Cervantes' fine qualities, it is his forgetfulness of this man who was capable of serving him even to martyrdom. But perhaps Miguel never knew his name. Perhaps he needed only to look into the man's eyes and see his loyalty reflected there.

He was a poor Moor whose name history has not handed down to us. One day they seized him, on his way to Oran, because he was carrying a letter from a Christian, requesting the help of his brethren to release him from his captivity. They took this letter away from him, and put him to death by impaling him. In his extremity, he refused to say, even under promise of pardon, from whose hands he had received the paper which meant his ruin. In his blessed innocence, he did not realise that the name for which they asked him was signed there, and he died without letting it pass his lips.

Perhaps that unconsecrated saint, Jorge del Olivar, was present at his death. Perhaps he raised his hand, trembling with emotion, in blessing on the dying man, and besought Heaven on his behalf, like that other unconsecrated saint conceived by a poet :

" Jesus, my God, what share in Thy glory dost Thou reserve for those who are good, even though they do not believe in Thee ? "

CHAPTER XI

FOR this fresh attempt at escape, Hassan sentenced Miguel de Cervantes to receive two thousand lashes; but this punishment, which would certainly have killed him, was not carried into effect.

Petitions from leading Moors, who knew and respected the famous captive, joined hands with requests for clemency from influential renegades, such as Maltrapillo the Murcian. The covetousness of the Pasha, who did not want to lose the ransom money, and his involuntary admiration for this man who so arrogantly defied death, played their part too. So Miguel did not share in the dreadful end which, at this time and for the same reason, was suffered by the Mallorcan Pedro Soler and Juan Vizcaíno.

At the beginning of the year 1579, when he had now been four years in captivity, Cervantes made the acquaintance of the Granadine Girón, a renegade who had taken the name of Abderrhaman. Miguel's conversation gently found its way to this new Mussulman's heart. It was wrung by the evocation of Miguel's quiet voice. The magic of Miguel's words called up in the renegade's memory scenes of far-off days: the flower gardens of Granada, a riot of carnations, with the white outline of the Sierra Nevada in the background; the fruit gardens of Toledo, amid whose fragrance brooks zigzagged to fall into the Tagus; the plains of Castile, smitten by the sun, where austere roses, like those of the holy poets, flowered amid thorns.

Abderrhaman felt that he would like to be Girón of

Granada once more. He got into touch with a Valencian merchant, named Onofre Exarque, resident in Algiers. With these two, Cervantes planned a fresh attempt at escape —his fourth. Questioned after its failure, he declared—and this statement of his is supported by Alonso Aragonés —that it was his own inspiration.

The plan consisted in fitting out an armed frigate which was to sail on a pretended corsair cruise, under the command of Abderrhaman. Exarque was to advance the money, which would amount to some seven hundred escudos. At the risk of his life, Pedro Girón was to lend the authority of his name of Abderrhaman to the enterprise.

We may well find it a matter for surprise, in these degenerate days of ours, when nobody either gives or lends money, life or conscience, except as a huckster and in hope of gain, that these men should have acted in this way. The Valencia merchant was ready to sacrifice a good part of his fortune, simply for the sake of serving God and his king. He could hope for no return, except as the sequel to a hazardous undertaking, in which he would adventure his own life, hitherto tranquil and safe. Pedro Girón was ready to leave the comfort and wealth of his home in Algiers, and go in search of penance and poverty in his distant homeland, just because his conscience smote him with the memory of the sufferings of the Man of Golgotha.

Cervantes informed his friends, and it was arranged that about seventy of them should sail in Onofre Exarque's ship.

The vessel was already purchased: a frigate with two banks of oars and a good ship under sail. Their hopes, too, scudded under crowded canvas, marking out the path over the sea which the ship was to follow.

" All were happy and contented, seeing how prosperously matters were going forward up to this point," says Alonso Aragonés.

But among those who were acquainted with Miguel's plan was a Dominican, a captive of Hassan Pasha's, who bore a deceptive name : Blanco de Paz.[1]

In his first attempt at escape, Miguel was deserted by the Moor who guided him; but this Moor was no traitor, nor had he anything to gain by his denunciation. He fled because his heart faltered at the thought of punishment. In Miguel's third attempt, it was similarly a Moor who helped him, and this unfortunate confidant of his died in horrible suffering without ever pronouncing Miguel's name.

It was in his second and fourth attempts that he found traitors his stumbling-block, and these two traitors had both received the waters of baptism. The first Judas was the Gilder, that twofold renegade. The other was Father Juan Blanco de Paz, of the Order of Saint Dominic, who was a renegade not to his liturgy, but to his faith as an honest man—if, indeed, he ever was one.

Blanco de Paz may have been invited by some of Cervantes' friends to take part in the attempt, or he may have been informed of it confidentially in his capacity as confessor. In any case, he arranged with a Florentine renegade that, through his medium, the plans of the captives should come to the ears of the viceroy.

Hassan, once advised about the project, concealed his knowledge of it, so that that fat fish Exarque, who had money hidden in his coffers and ships which sailed the seas, should fall into his net. To the Dominican Judas, as a reward

[1] Literally, " White of Peace " (Translator's note).

for his vileness, he sent a gold escudo and a jar of butter. Perhaps the friar expected his thirty pieces of silver; but Hassan regarded him as so despicable, so mean, that he was not worthy to be compared with Judas even in his pay.

Among the conspirators the news soon spread that their plans were unmasked. Exarque feared lest Miguel, put to the torture, should disclose his complicity in the plot, with the result that he might lose his fortune and even his life. To conjure away this danger, he suggested to Miguel that he should pay the price of his ransom himself, and that Miguel should leave for Spain in the first ship sailing there.

But Cervantes refused, and gently reproached Exarque for his doubts of him. He could not accept liberty for himself alone, when so many people who looked forward to liberty through him would have to be left behind. Nobody else need fear punishment, which would fall on his own head alone, since he, Miguel de Cervantes, was the sole author of the plan, and, even in the last extremity, he would never soil his lips by accusing anybody else. Onofre Exarque need not lament the prospect of losing his liberty, or even his money; for no proof against him existed except such proof as might issue from the mouth of Miguel de Cervantes, and he would bite off his own tongue if ever he felt upon it, like an eruption of sores, the syllables of the name of a friend.

Don Diego de Castellanos, one of those who were to have escaped with Miguel, advised him to go into hiding. This would give the viceroy's anger time to tire. The royal wrath, when it overtook him, would be jaded and spent, and so deal less harshly with him. Castellanos himself found a refuge for him. There Miguel spent a few days.

But a proclamation by the viceroy, threatening with death anybody who held Cervantes concealed and did not deliver him up, induced Miguel to present himself before the despot. He sought out the shipmaster Maltrapillo, a renegade exceptionally kindly among those of his breed; and Maltrapillo, who was a friend of Hassan's and in his confidence, accompanied Miguel to the viceroy's palace.

Once again, Cervantes' valiant soul, his contempt for pain and death, astonished the viceroy of Algiers. Once again, we see his spirit soaring in lofty flight above all human littleness. It was as though, at this moment, his soul escaped from his body, ascended into Heaven, and received from the Universal Light itself those rays which were later to halo his brow with genius and be reflected in his immortal pages.

Cervantes suffered insult. He felt around his neck the rope which might end his life. He saw around him the threatening faces of the executioners.

Nothing daunted him. His soul had soared so high that perhaps it did not understand what pain and death meant, because it was so far above them. Not a single name issued from his lips except his own.

" I alone, Miguel de Cervantes, am he who concocted this plot. Nobody knew anything about my plans, and, if anybody helped me, he is already far away and free."

It was his last moment of greatness; of magnificence not bestowed upon him by life, but wrested from life by his strength of soul.

Afterwards, life sought to be revenged on him who had conquered it with so gallant a gesture. It was to drag him along in its hard hands. It was to put him under the harrow of misfortune, poverty, and neglect. In the end, it was to throw him away, beaten and broken, in a mean corner. Thence, a new Job in his patience and his lamentation, he was to beseech the great in a plaintive voice—and seldom did they listen to him—for a crumb of patronage, in return for a diamond rarer than the richest of their jewels.

CHAPTER XII

HE spent five hard months of imprisonment, shackled with gyves and fetters in a Moorish dungeon. Then, at last, the day of liberty dawned for him.

Out of all the captive gentlemen compromised in this last attempt at escape, out of all those who had lent it their support, only Miguel had been made to suffer, to purge his sin of greatness of soul. The merchant Exarque got off scot-free, because nothing could be proved against him, and the renegade Girón was merely banished to Tetuan by way of punishment.

Out of all of them, only Miguel suffered hunger and thirst for justice, even if he did not suffer the physical pangs of hunger and thirst. . . .

But, one flowery May day, out of flowery Valencia, there sailed for Algiers a ship aboard which travelled two Trinitarian monks: Father Juan Gil and Fray Antonio de la Bella. He bore a sweet name, this latter monk, and it was not a deceptive one like that of Blanco de Paz. It foreshadowed the holy mission that was entrusted to him: La Bella, the beautiful. So those who endure its loss will ever call liberty—liberty the beautiful

> " Whiter and more lovely
> Than April meadow full of flowers."

For there can be no pleasure if it is not sweetened by the honey of freedom.

On the twenty-ninth day of May, the ship entered the

port of Algiers, and during the months of June and July more than two hundred captives were ransomed. In August Fray Antonio returned to Spain with one hundred and eight of them. Father Gil stayed in Algiers.

He had a special mission: the freeing of a captive about whose large heart, whose heroic soul, high praises were sung by all those who had known him in the prisons of Algiers. But, above all, the friar bore with him the remembrance of a mother's tears which had bathed his hands.

Doña Leonor de Cortinas had given him all the money she had, together with what she had been able to obtain from the royal treasury. Her daughters had helped her; but among them all, even counting the aid of a pious bequest, they could not assemble the five hundred ducats which Hassan demanded for the release of Miguel de Cervantes.

But this was not the only difficulty which the Trinitarian Father had to face in accomplishing his mission. First of all, he had to find the captive. Only after he had found Miguel, in a wretched state in his dungeon without air or light, could he attempt, by dint of good words, to shatter the hardness of the viceroy's avaricious heart.

He failed in this attempt. Their negotiations dragged on until Hassan's mandate expired. The Grand Turk had designated Jafer Pasha as viceroy of Algiers, and Hassan had to set out for Constantinople.

On the nineteenth day of September of 1580, when the deposed viceroy's jewels, women, servants and slaves were already on board the ships which were to transport him,

Father Gil " sought among the merchants " for the two hundred and twenty ducats that were still lacking to make up the five hundred demanded by Hassan. At the last moment, out of all the viceroy's captives, one was disembarked who, according to the document drawn up and signed at that moment, was " a native of Madrid, of medium height, heavily bearded, with a maimed left hand and arm, captured in the galley *Sol*, on her way from Naples to Spain. . . ."

At last Miguel de Cervantes was free, after five years in captivity.

With the first steps he was able to take without dragging a chain along with him, he hastened to thank that good Trinitarian Father who had devoted so many comings and goings, so many prayers and petitions, to his service.

Juan Gil doubtless believed that—apart from the reward which the sum of all his sacrifices would gain for him at his last hour—this good deed of his would win him no greater reward than the gratitude of a poor maimed man and a few weeping women. As he signed the certificate of release, with a hand trembling with the joy of helping a fellow-man, he could not tell that he was carving his name, stroke by stroke and letter by letter, among the names of the immortals.

Before he set out for Spain, Miguel would also have liked to thank the Valencian merchant, Exarque, who had shown himself so generous with his money and his peace of mind. But fear of compromising Exarque once more halted his steps on the threshold of the merchant's shop.

F

For a whole month, and for the first time, Miguel was now free to go where he would about the streets of Algiers. For the first time, he could sit down at his ease to chat with his friends and eat his meals in peace.

Never before had he been able to linger as he could now, with such delight in feasting his eyes upon new things, in front of the shops of the vendors of Persian carpets and Aleppo pottery, who gravely smoked their narghiles, letting the hours pass by them without troubling to follow them in their flight; or in front of the Christian shops whose owners, like the Spaniard Exarque, came under safe conduct of the viceroy to ply their trade in cosmo-politan Algiers: Englishmen who dealt in bone, lead and copper ware; Valencians and Catalans who offered pearls, painted fabrics, and wine; Provençals who sold steel and sulphur; Genovese and Neapolitan vendors of silks and velvets; Venetians who displayed their little carved coffers and their marvellously diaphanous mirrors.

In one of these bazaars he once had to take refuge when the Mahalas galloped down the street on their chargers, on their way back from the interior, where they had gone to levy taxes for the Grand Turk and, incidentally, rob any caravans they met on their way.

Never before had he been able to surrender, as he could now, to the spell of the silent corners of the Moorish city, and its narrow streets, whose houses thrust their latticed bay-windows forward as though they were seeking to kiss one another and rob the sky of its horizon: which, indeed, amounts to robbery of lovers, who believe that the sky was made for themselves.

Behind some lattice, there might be dark eyes on the watch. Perhaps Miguel knew already what those eyes looked like; but he never told us.

If, in his story of the "captive," as in other stories which he wrote, there is something of his own love life, it is not in his own boasting, but in our own conjecture, that we have to find evidence of it. Cervantes kept his heart to himself, and did not wear it on his sleeve, as so many other people did in his own time, and as so many do in ours.

Doubtless he felt that in offering us the fruits of his mind he was doing enough to win him our admiration and affection. Nowhere does he tell us how that Neapolitan son of his, whom he describes for us in his *Journey to Parnassus*, and that Isabel de Saavedra, who was to be an embitterment rather than a consolation of his old age, came into the world.

But we are entitled to assume that the man who risked his life so many times, and with such gallantry, to win his liberty, was not backward in adventuring it for that other thing which is as dear and desirable as liberty itself, namely, love.

Some seraglio may have known his cautious steps. Soft, white hands may have left in his red beard the perfumed memory of caressing fingers. Perhaps, once more, he was ready to risk the life and liberty which he had but now regained for just one moment of love, just one murmur, within beloved arms, of that sweet Arab song, learned on some moonlit night:

"I took leave of her, and, while my left hand clasped her waist, my right hand brushed away my tears."

83

And she would answer him in the words of that other song, which holds all the heart-break of absence :

"My heart awaits you, O wanderer! To what lands unknown have you gone; in what city, in what house, have you found shelter?

"At what spring do you drink, O wanderer? I, who weep for you, feed upon the roses of my memory. I quench my thirst at the abundant fountain of my eyes."

Miguel gossiped in the pleasant company of Doctor Sosa, who was very fond of him, and Father Gil, his liberator. He sat down to table at a farewell banquet to those who had been the comrades of his bitterness and his hopes. They talked about absent friends, about those who had sailed for Turkey in Hassan's ship, such as Sánchez de Alcaudete the Cordovan, Jaime de Latasa, Pedro de Biedma, who had taken part in his attempts at escape; and, above all, Don Jerónimo de Palafox, that mirror of chivalry, whom Father Gil had tried so hard to ransom, only to encounter the stumbling-block of Hassan's greed.

In the course of these conversations, it came to Cervantes' knowledge that that despicable friar, Blanco de Paz, was stirring up envy and hatred against him, and trying to forfeit him the good opinion in which he was held. The Dominican set himself up as delegate of the Inquisition in Algiers, since he had been so in Spain during the days of his liberty. He appointed himself judge and jailer of consciences, with no better title than his own ill will—though, for that matter, he was just the man to be a myrmidon of the Holy Office.

He outdid himself in defamatory dispatches to the ports of Spain, to the end that they should be closed against the man who had sighed for so long to return to them; or to ensure that, if they welcomed him, it should be with all the panoply of an *auto-da-fe*.

But the good Father Gil was ready to meet him with testimony to the exemplary life which Cervantes had led during his captivity; and he was supported by the worthy Don Antonio de Sosa and all Miguel's comrades, such as Ensign Diego Castellanos, Alonso Aragonés, Villalon, and many others who hastened to testify to what was the truth, to their own knowledge: the probity, the worth and the fortitude of Miguel de Cervantes.

At the end of his testimony, Father Gil delivers himself of this weighty reproof to the viperous tongue of the infamous Dominican:

" I have spoken and conversed and been on intimate and familiar terms with the said Miguel de Cervantes, on whose behalf I present this information; and I know him to be highly esteemed as a servant of Your Majesty for many years; and especially during the course of his captivity he has done things for which Your Majesty owes him much gratitude, as the evidence attached herewith testifies more fully. *And if he were not such in his actions and behaviour, and if he were not reputed and regarded as such by all, I should never have admitted him to my friendship and intimacy....*"

The hatred of Blanco de Paz for a man who had never done him any harm is not easily to be explained—unless it was a mortal sin for Miguel to be understanding and kindly towards all those whose hearts and wills failed them. The Dominican friar stayed in Algiers. He had to suffer the mortification of being impotent to do Cervantes any harm and witnessing the departure, at once a source of regret and of congratulation on all hands, of the man whom he hated so bitterly, and whose good fortune hurt him even worse than his own misfortune.

85

On the twenty-fourth day of October, thirty-six days after his ransoming, Miguel de Cervantes embarked in Antón Francés' ship. It was a small ship, which traded between Africa and the eastern ports of Spain.

With Cervantes sailed two great friends of his, Rodrigo de Chaves and Diego de Benavides. The latter was under great obligations to our gentleman of Alcalá. He describes Cervantes as having been so good to him "that in him, strange as I was to the country, I found a father and a mother."

Miguel gazed at the sea over which he was sailing north-westwards. He did not yet know at what port of life his ship would land him.

His taste for literature was by now almost forgotten. One or two attempts at plays, written more for his own amusement than with any hope of gain, and a few stories of pastoral life, scarcely more than an outlet for his home-sickness, through which he could look from the darkness of his prison upon the bright landscapes he had seen in better days—these were his whole production during these past five years.

Doubtless the path of the soldier, upon which he had stumbled by chance in the labyrinth of his days, was the one that he would have to follow. In spite of his maimed arm, he had plenty of vigour left; and, if the career of letters sounded a sweeter summons to him, it did not promise to remedy his poverty. Those gallant doings of his in captivity, attested by so many irrefutable witnesses, together with the record of his brave bearing at Lepanto, would serve his turn better.

But the ship pursued her north-westerly course, as though

she were a symbol, an arrow sped by an augur's hand to reveal his destiny.

North: low down on the horizon, on clear nights, he could see a little star shining, towards which the compass kept its needle eternally pointed. Miguel sought his true north, too, all his life long, with his desires set upon a goal which still shone in the distance, hidden though it might be, from time to time, by storm and fog.

At last, on this soft autumn night, the star seemed to shine clearly, and the ship ran towards it without wavering, straight as a dart, with a fair wind in her sails. But, all at once, the ship changed her course towards the west.

West: already Miguel's life, after shining at its zenith in his captivity, was sinking to its setting. It was to be a life dim and obscure, upon which little men who came in contact with it could look without its light blinding them, and pass by on the other side with a disdainful gesture, like those grandees to whom he dedicated his works; a life whose light was to be quenched by the brightness of other stars, such as Lope de Vega; a life whose light unimportant but audacious people, such as Avellaneda, sought to hide by lighting their own wretched little candles in imitation of it.

Another time was to come, closer to his last years, when, as he opened the window of his soul, he could feel the breath of popularity upon his face. But then it was to be too late to remedy the sorrows of that life of his which was bitter, if not embittered; nor were his straitened circumstances to be remedied by the whiff of fame. His life was to end with one day just like the next, with no brightness, with no sufficiency, despite that inner splendour of his which was later to blind us.

It was only when he was dead that we were to see his glory in all its clarity, as though it had been enclosed in the dark vessel of his body, and only when that vessel was shattered could it escape from its sheath.

CHAPTER XIII

ANTON FRANCES' ship arrived at Denia at the end of October, after a good voyage.

From Denia, the ransomed captives set off for Valencia, into which city they entered in solemn procession, to the accompaniment of kettle-drums and flageolets, bare-headed and in the humble garments which recalled their slavery, while ragamuffins sold sightseers, for a few maravedies, copies of *The true story of the captives ransomed this year,* which the Redemptorist Fathers had printed for the benefit of the liberated men.

When the ceremony of their entrance was over—it included a mournful sermon with which the Catholic Church welcomed her sons redeemed from " the oppressive power of the barbarian "—the late captives were now entirely free to take, out of all the roads of Spain, whatever one seemed good to them.

Miguel, as a matter of fact, spent some days—perhaps the whole of November—in Valencia. From this city he wrote to his family telling them the good news of his arrival, and also asking them to send him money for his journey home, if they were in a position to do so after all the sacrifices they had made to obtain his ransom. He further requested them to make a fresh statement before a notary of his merits in war and captivity, so that the reward which they deserved might be waiting for him on his arrival in Madrid.

Mateo Vázquez, in whose friendship he trusted, had become first secretary of His Majesty Don Philip, now that the King had summoned up courage to imprison Antonio Pérez, accused by public opinion of being Escobedo's assassin. Miguel believed that with Vázquez's influence, and the support of the testimonials he carried with him, he would secure appointment to the command of a company, as had been promised him, six years before, by His Serene Highness Don John, now dead in the States of Flanders, heart-broken by grief and despair.

During his stay in the Valencian capital, he visited his good friends who resided in that city, and those whom he had known in Algiers or with whom he had come into contact during his attempts at escape : the saintly Jorge del Olivar, the generous Exarque and Torres and Fortuni. From them he learnt how things were going in Castile.

Philip II was on the frontier of Portugal with a strong army commanded by the Duke of Alba, who, in the critical circumstances of the moment, had been taken back into the King's confidence. The impetuous Dom Sebastian, King of Portugal, had fallen fighting the Moors in Africa, and his great-uncle, the Cardinal Dom Henry, had succeeded him for a few months on the throne of Portugal.

Of no avail was the desire of the old King-Cardinal, if his seventy-seven years would allow him, to give a little king to Portugal and so found a new dynasty. In Rome there were faithful emissaries of the Catholic King of Spain who opposed Dom Henry's plans, and Pope Sixtus V, then on the friendliest terms with the Court of Madrid, refused the Cardinal a dispensation which would enable him to marry.

Don Cristóbal de Moura, sent by Philip, had gone to Lisbon, and there put daily obstacles in the old Portuguese

King's path. Moura's object was to wear away his hold on the crown and even on life, and make an end of him. The poor old man, who had never expected to shoulder such responsibilities and was in no way prepared for them, had finally fallen in with Moura's wishes and breathed his last sigh, one fine spring day in this same year of 1580.

Now the King of Spain had no rival in his claim to the crown of Portugal except the Prior of Ocrato, who had Jewish blood in him. He was reputed to be a grandson of Manoel the Great; though, if those who claimed to be well informed were to be believed, there was a break in the direct line, and the royal blood of Dom Manoel, thanks to irregular lapses, did not run in the veins of this pretender to the throne.

If these palace whisperings were to be disregarded, then perhaps Dom Antonio, Prior of Ocrato, as the descendant of the Portuguese kings in the direct male line, had a better title to the crown of Portugal than Don Philip of Austria, also a grandson of Dom Manoel, but in the female line. But rights hasten to take cover in the presence of facts, when these facts speak loudly and clearly enough; or allow themselves to be ousted by the wiles, the caresses and the gifts of Dame Diplomacy.

The Duke of Alba, the tamer of the States of Flanders, was at the gates of Portugal with a powerful army. Meanwhile, Moura loaded presents on poor Portuguese, and threats on timid ones, with the result that they soon came to see that Don Philip alone was the legitimate heir to Dom Sebastian the impetuous and Dom Henry the Cardinal.

With the Court of Spain, which had transferred itself to

Badajoz, was Mateo Vázquez, upon whom Miguel based his hopes.

Affairs in Portugal were settled thanks to the efforts of the envoy Moura, the Duke of Alba and his lieutenant Sancho de Ávila. Meanwhile the Court went into mourning for the death of Doña Anne of Austria, Philip's fourth wife, which took place in the frontier province of Estremadura, in such mysterious circumstances that it has been attributed to various causes.

The one which most honours the memory of husband and wife is that the Queen voluntarily offered herself to the saints of Heaven, so that it might be she, and not her husband—fallen sick of some unknown disease—who should leave the tribulations of this world. The one which most dishonours their memory is that the Queen died as the result of blows from her royal, but bad-tempered spouse— the sequel to a dispute about a will.

Meanwhile, Miguel set out for Madrid to embrace his family, and to see whether his own affairs would get on as well as those of the new King of Portugal, and whether the veteran maimed at Lepanto could get himself a captaincy of troops at the same time as the Emperor Charles V's son got himself a new crown.

But Philip II was better served than Miguel de Cervantes. Moura was a master of the art of intrigue and persuasion, and Alba and Ávila knew how to take by force what was not to be won by goodwill. Lisbon and Oporto groaned under the excesses of their soldiery, who followed the example set by the Duke himself in the fields and the cities of Flanders, in the way of attaching no undue importance to the sanctity of life, property or virginity.

Otherwise we should not find Don Fernando Álvarez de Toledo—an old man, near to death and to his reckoning with God, and also more closely related to the Portuguese than to the Flemings—reproving the violence of the soldiers and castigating it with so heavy a hand as he did.

"The disorder which is now taking place," he wrote in a letter to the King,

> "is such as I could never have imagined, and such as is not to be admitted among men-at-arms. I assure Your Majesty that there is no colonel, major, captain or any other officer who does his duty as he ought to do it, and that all of them might just as well be relieved of their commissions. I have hanged a fair number of soldiers; I have sent some fifty to the galleys; I have suspended eight captains from their duties, and I feel like suspending all of them. I have hanged, and I keep on hanging, so many marauders that I am afraid of running out of rope."

The good Don Fernando, old and ailing though he might be, clearly did not fall far behind his leader in heaviness of hand; but he felt that he was using it to the greater glory of God, into Whose presence he might be summoned at any moment. Sancho de Ávila did not worry about such niceties. He simply hanged partisans of Dom Antonio who fell into the hands of the Spanish troops, and gave towns over to sack by his soldiery.

In Oporto the churches and monasteries where jewels were kept for the adornment of relics and altars were regarded as fair prize. "Not a crucifix or a chalice was left in the whole district," Sancho de Ávila himself admits.

Miguel de Cervantes could not storm and sack palace ante-rooms in order to take by force what was not granted him willingly. He had to resign himself—like so many other veterans whose wounds were now healed, just as men's memories were sealed against the occasion of them—to begging for a favour and waiting for it patiently and humbly.

In this dreary occupation he spent all the latter days of 1580 and the early days of 1581. In the spring of this year Miguel set off for Portugal, where his brother Rodrigo was serving in Don Lope de Figueroa's *tercio*. With him went his good friend and comrade in captivity, Rodrigo de Chaves.

But return to the army, which was an easy solution for many veterans of the wars of Flanders, Africa and Italy, was not so easy in Miguel's case, for there was great competition and he was handicapped by his maimed left hand.

At one time it was believed that he took part in the Marquis of Santa Cruz's naval expedition for the relief of the island of Terceira in the Azores, which had been captured by Dom Antonio with the help of a French squadron under the command of Philip Strozzi. There is no better foundation for this belief than the following passage in his petition for a grant, written in 1590, which recalled the joint services of the two brothers Rodrigo and Miguel: " After their liberation, they proceeded to serve Your Majesty in the Kingdom of Portugal and Terceira under the Marquis of Santa Cruz."

But this is probably applicable only to Miguel's brother Rodrigo. No distinction is drawn in this document between the two expeditions of 1582 and 1583, and Miguel could not have taken part in the second, for there is another document, and a sad one, which proves that he was in Madrid at that time.

94

In May of 1581 Miguel was in Lisbon and at Thomar. At Thomar the King had convoked the Portuguese Cortes for the purpose of crowning him. The fortunate claimant was followed in his progress by an unfortunate claimant.

Miguel did not obtain the captaincy of his dreams. He had to content himself with a mission to the authorities at Oran which was entrusted to him at this time. It was only a temporary job, but by now Miguel had to cut the coat of his hopes to the measure of this poor piece of cloth.

Lope Giner, paymaster of the royal fleet at Cartagena, received an order, dated from Thomar, to pay Miguel de Cervantes fifty ducats by way of an advance on one hundred ducats for expenses, " in consideration of the fact that he is proceeding in connection with a certain matter in the royal service." The other fifty ducats he was to receive through Juan Fernández de Espinosa, the royal treasurer, on his return from his voyage.

We know nothing about what dispatches he carried to Oran or what was the nature of his mission. He spent a month on the voyage, and returned to Lisbon, in search of further employment.

By this time the Portuguese capital had submitted to the yoke of Philip, and its inhabitants could move peacefully about the streets without fear of being attacked or despoiled. Miguel mingled with the crowd along the banks of the Tagus, enjoying the fine landscape, bathed by the sea and the light of the setting sun.

These river shores reached by the Ocean remained in his memory, and he wanted those of us who could not visit them to enjoy their charm. His *Galatea*—perhaps far advanced by this time—recalls them in a fine passage, in which he speaks of clear, resplendent skies, and the union of eternal spring with lovely Venus in her girded garment of love. He speaks, too, of " leafy groves of gentle olive, verdant laurel, tufted myrtle. . . ."

There is such smoothness, such rhythm in these sentences of his, their sylvan metre is so deliberate as to suggest—as the most distinguished of his commentators has noted—that he began the work as poetry, and only afterwards turned it into prose: but his own prose, which, after all, is worth as much as the most limpid and harmonious of poetry.

HOUSE WHERE CERVANTES LIVED IN VALLADOLID

CHAPTER XIV

On his return to Madrid from Lisbon, where he obtained no more recompense for his services than that ephemeral employment as a dispatch carrier, he found nothing but straitened circumstances in his parents' home and forgetfulness on the part of those whom he still believed were bound to reward him.

It was by now the middle of the year 1583. Rodrigo had stayed behind in Portugal with his *tercio*, in readiness for a fresh disembarkation in the Azores, where the Spanish troops, in the course of the summer, were to make a bloody end of the Prior of Ocrato's insurrection.

The only trace which remains to us of Miguel's stay in the Spanish capital at this time, while the expedition to the island of Terceira was in progress, is one record more of his penury.

About this time his sister Andrea received a splendid present from the Italian Leocadelo, " because, in his absence from his hearth and home, she had been kind to him and nursed him through sickness." She came to the help of her impoverished family at the beginning of September by pawning a part of his gift : " five hangings of taffeta, yellow and coloured, for the adornment of a room." It was Miguel who executed his sister's commission and received from the hands of the pawnbroker Napoleon Lomelin the thirty ducats which he advanced.

Miguel's life during these months from 1583 to 1584 is obscure. He had finished with the career of arms, and the point of his pen had not yet, like a chick's beak, pierced the shell of anonymity. His sole occupation, if he had to state one in formal documents, was that of " resident in the capital."

He frequented the gossip-centres of Madrid. Everybody was talking about the trial of Antonio Pérez and the Princess of Eboli, the arrogant way in which they answered their judges, and the ostentatious style in which they lived. Rodrigo Mangado, Dom Antonio's squire, and the astrologer Pedro de la Hera both died about this time. It was common talk that they died of a surfeit of things they knew about Escobedo's assassination. Antonio Pérez, so it was said, had sought to relieve them with a purge which dispatched them to the next world, where their conversation would be less bad for his own health than it was in this one.

Miguel also kicked his heels in the ante-chambers of those who dispensed favours. But claimants were many, and prizes did not go to those who were the most deserving, but to those who bowed and scraped the lowest and had the knack of turning a complimentary phrase just at the right moment.

The number of the fabled plagues of Egypt had been increased by this plague of heroes who sprang up on the fields of battle and then came in swarms to devastate the wheat of the treasury. But the royal coffers were suffering from such bad harvests that the king himself had to be content not with a plentiful reaping, but with a mere gleaning of the impoverished fields.

With less and less illusions about his prospects, in proportion as the epic occasion of Lepanto, which he had hoped would mean his advancement, fell further and further behind, Miguel de Cervantes paraded his patience and his maimed hand about the capital, awaiting better times. By now he based his hopes, not upon the captaincy of which he had once dreamed, but on some humbler employment. He could not obtain even that.

Finally he renewed an old friendship with a family living in Esquivias, in which there was a marriageable daughter with a dowry not to be despised. Miguel was now going on for thirty-seven, and the Castilian girl was not yet twenty. But the advice of his family impelled the weather-beaten veteran towards the girl, who knew nothing about the world outside the dusty streets of Esquivias.

Miguel had to break off another love affair in order to make a success of this one. He had a mistress, Anna de Rojas, or Anna Franca, an attractive, easy-going girl. In her arms the poor maimed man had found consolation for his troubles and forgetfulness of his disappointments.

Their relations had already been complicated by the birth of a daughter, who was given the name of Isabel, to which was added that of Saavedra, a gift from her father. But, when the time arrived for Miguel's marriage with the provincial girl, Doña Catalina de Palacios, the good Anna Franca vanished into smoke. She effaced herself from his life, lest she should stand in the way of his good fortune, if her leaving him was the only means by which he could attain it.

Anna Franca herself got married, after Cervantes' marriage, to one Alonso Rodríguez, who, though he may have had other misfortunes, did not suffer in any way from the terrible tortures of jealousy. This Alonso Rodríguez was probably the same manager and producer of plays who at this time was touring the playhouses of Castile with his strolling troupe. If so, Anna Franca may have been a lady of the theatre, an actress who tramped the dusty roads dressed as a queen.

Such momentary greatness was doubtless all that Isabel de Saavedra's mother ever enjoyed, despite the rich appurtenances of a very great lady with which she has been invested in the imagination of some biographers of Cervantes. Poor Miguel, who had now lost the good looks and the proud bearing of his early years, and was by no means well dressed, can scarcely have been in a position to frequent ladies of high degree. He is much more likely to have become intimate with a strolling player, a class of girl with whom he must often have come in contact, addicted as he was to the company of actors and actresses.

By the end of 1584 Miguel was ready to wed the damsel of Esquivias. Meanwhile he had constantly covered the six leagues which separated the capital from the Toledan village, just for the sake of a talk with Doña Catalina de Palacios. Doubtless the opposition of her family, clearly shown by their absence from the wedding, closed the doors of the house against our gentleman of Alcalá, and the betrothed pair had to talk through one of the gratings which are still to be seen in its earthen walls.

Miguel's heart, though it may first have been impelled towards the girl by the hand of convenience, was now really attracted by her youth and her witty conversation. It leapt for joy when the smooth line of the horizon of La Mancha was broken by the gentle green undulation of the low hills called after Santa Barbara. The village nestled at their foot, and Miguel tried to make out, in the medley of old grey houses, the one in which he was awaited with such sweet impatience.

Doña Catalina's father was dead. It was her clerical brother, Don Francisco de Palacios, who, with a wealth of argument, headed the opposition to his sister's marriage with this hero at a loose end, maimed and no longer young.

Miguel was mortified by the small esteem in which he was held by his betrothed's relations. It aroused in him a just desire to repay, one by one, all the wounds which their gossiping tongues inflicted on him. The hand which was to cast their darts back at them was to prove that of a man who, sound only in one hand though he might be, was unique among the geniuses of Spain. While the darts of the Palacios, the Salazares and the Quijadas did not fly beyond the fences of their farmyards, those which he launched were to traverse all the ages in endless flight.

But Miguel did not dare to aim point-blank at the priest, lest he should come into collision with the Church again. He launched his darts against a lean and shrivelled squireling, by name Alonso Quijada, who, although he was at odds with the Palacios over a matter of business, was not the most behindhand in jeering at his cousin's marriage.

Many years afterwards, there was to be held up for public entertainment one Alonso Quijada or Quijano, living in a village " whose name " the author " did not choose to remember," on account of the many unpleasantnesses which he experienced there at the time of his marriage. This country squire made his appearance, in his creator's primary intention, merely for the amusement of those who should read the story of his comical misadventures.

Cervantes intended simply to make the name of Alonso

Quijano a laughing-stock, and to have him followed in the future by a retinue of guffaws. But many years had gone by since the time of the affront, and Cervantes' resentment had sweetened within him. Because he was old, like wine he had turned generous. No longer did he want to treat the figure of his knight mercilessly. Instead, in his closing pages, he called him " the Good."

He laughed at his own invention, and he wanted other people to laugh too ; but this good Don Alonso did not issue from his pen so badly used as was doubtless his first intention. Cervantes had kept him so long in his own mind that he had become his own creation, and he caressed him gently and lovingly before he sent him forth on the roads of La Mancha.

But neither did Cervantes realise that, in his figure of this crazy fellow, he was creating the most superbly, the most pitifully human of all the literary figures that any pen had ever created. In the first part of the book, above all, he had merely the humble intention of writing a work for the amusement of the few. His genius forged a masterpiece upon which the whole world was to meditate.

Cervantes wrote the unimportant name of Alonso Quijada at the beginning of his *Don Quixote* because he never expected that it was to be carried on the wings of the wind, to the accompaniment of a murmur of praise, uphill and down dale, to the most remote of cities. He himself put into the mouth of Rocinante the judgment which he believed Don Quixote's craziness and Sancho's simplicity would merit in the eyes of his readers :

> " Why should I complain of my sorrows,
> When my master and his squire or majordomo
> Are as sorry as his sorry nag ? "

In any case, the opposition of the cleric, Don Alonso, and other relations of the bride, if it embittered hours which should have been sweet, did not prevent the wedding. In the course of their long talks together, the damsel of Esquivias had gradually learned all about the veteran's hard life, and she loved him for the risks he had run and the trials he had endured. More and more, in spite of all of them, she wanted to unite her humble life to the glorious life of Miguel de Cervantes.

About their love affair might have been written one of the finest pages of Miguel's contemporary and equal in loftiness of genius : William Shakespeare. Cervantes might have said, like Othello, that she

> " Still questioned me the story of my life
> From year to year, the battles, sieges, fortunes,
> That I have pass'd.
> I ran it through, even from my boyish days
> To the very moment . . ."

And when, from inside the house, some voice summoned her to domestic duties, Doña Catalina must have left her window and hurried to do what had to be done, hastily, feverishly, longing to go back soon and listen once more to the tale of adventure. . . .

> " But still the house affairs would draw her thence ;
> Which ever as she could with haste dispatch,
> She'd come again, and with a greedy ear
> Devour up my discourse. . . .
>
> And often did beguile her of her tears
> When I did speak of some distressful stroke
> That my youth suffered. . . ."

Cervantes too, like the Moor of Venice, felt himself beloved by his Desdemona as she listened to the story of his misadventures :

> " She loved me for the dangers I had pass'd,
> And I loved her that she did pity them."

CHAPTER XV

THEY were married on the 12th of December 1584. No relation of the bride was present at the wedding except her uncle, Don Juan Palacios, the curate of the parish, who celebrated the marriage.

As her dowry, Doña Catalina brought to it some olive groves and vineyards, and a share of furniture and farm implements, to the total value of one hundred and eighty-two thousand maravedies: a value which, in spite of its imposing hundreds of thousands, merely meant five thousand three hundred and fifty silver reales.[1] In this was included only her share in her inheritance from her father. When her mother died, the daughter would get considerably more, and she also had reason to believe that her uncle, the priest Don Juan, would leave her a legacy of some importance.

But by now Miguel himself was in a position to bring something to their nest to make it more comfortable. His *Galatea* had just been published from the presses of Blas de Robles, the Alcalá printer, who acquired the rights in the work for one thousand three hundred and thirty-six reales. This sum Cervantes received in the month of July, and doubtless much of it was spent upon the tailor's bills and Church dues which his marriage involved.

It has been said that his *Galatea* was the story of his

[1] The *real* was worth approximately 3¼d; but the value of money at the period must be multiplied several times to arrive at its modern equivalent. (Translator's note.)

love affair with Doña Catalina, served up in accordance with the pastoral taste which was the vogue at that time. But nothing more than the merest conjecture has been advanced in support of this assertion. It may be taken for granted that neither was Cervantes drawing a portrait of himself in the likeness of Elicio, "shepherd on the banks of the Tagus, to whom Nature showed herself as liberal as Fortune and Love were parsimonious"; nor was he depicting his Doña Catalina in these words:

"Peerless Galatea, shepherdess on those same banks born, who, though in that pastoral and rustic occupation reared, was so lofty and quick of mind that witty dames nurtured in royal palaces thought themselves fortunate to be her equal in any one thing, whether in wit or in beauty."

Cervantes had already begun, and indeed more or less finished, his *Galatea* when he met Doña Catalina—or, at least, if he had known her as a child, when he met her again as the girl of marriageable age who became his wife. For this work was not a sudden outburst of genius, dashed off in a few days or weeks. In it is to be discerned the hand of the artificer who polishes his sentences painstakingly, so that no roughness of language should jar upon the ear. Cervantes says himself in his prologue: "I have not published this book *before now*. . . ."

If any episodes were inspired by his visits to the Toledan village, they were fitted into the work like bits into a mosaic, more as a matter of taste and to make the whole more pleasing to the reader than from any organic necessity. Even so, it cannot be said that Catalina was one of the shepherdesses in Galatea's train.

That she may have been one can only be conjectured

from the fact that, when the first part was published about the time of his wedding, the author promised a second part, " for the reader's further entertainment and of better contriving," but never fulfilled this promise. Here alone can be found some ground for this risky assertion.

For Miguel's Doña Catalina was nothing like the Galatea of his dreams. She was not "lofty and quick of mind" and of a pretty wit, but extremely provincial in her tastes and manners. She never stopped looking back on past days at Esquivias, when she was still a girl and unmarried, the spoilt darling of her old mother and her uncle the priest.

Now, in the capital, whose life and customs jarred upon her because she was unfamiliar with them, her character deteriorated. She flared readily into fits of bad temper. On the smallest pretext she went back to her village, in search of maternal kisses and the avuncular horselaughs that echoed through the house; while Miguel stayed in Madrid, bereft of affection, with a wife alive but remote from his heart and hearth, which is a widowerhood more sorrowful than that of death.

Doña Catalina proved nothing like her whom Miguel had imagined as the sweet heroine of his eclogue. If he ever happened to have any intention of drawing her portrait in the first part of his *Galatea*, he changed his model in such a way that nobody would ever know her. He went back once more to the imaginary fields of his book, where all the shepherds had fine bearing and courteous manners, and all the shepherdesses had complexions of milk and roses, and talked in fine language and polished periods.

The book is frankly a conceit; but the times preferred imaginativeness to realism, and it soon won more popular approval than its elder brothers, the *Dianas* by Montemayor and Gaspar Gil Polo, Montalvo's *Felida's Shepherd*, and that mother of them all which came to Spain from Italy, introduced by Sannazaro, under the name of *Arcadia*.

Miguel de Cervantes was to be known for many years as the author of *Galatea*, until, one day, there came from the printing presses the book which was to make all the other books of its author forgotten, and even those of many other authors. In this mature fruit of his genius, Cervantes was to show himself a sincere critic of its first-fruits. In connection with the " curious and profound scrutiny which the priest and the barber made of the library of our ingenuous knight," he says, referring to his own *Galatea*: " A book not so badly constructed, but one which suggests something and gets nowhere. One would have to await its promised second part."

He is warmer in his praise of *Felida's Shepherd* and *Angelica's Tears*: books over which the priest would have wept if he had had to order them to be committed to the flames. But neither Montalvo's work nor that of Luis Barahona de Soto stuck in people's memories like his own *Galatea*, which " suggests something and gets nowhere."

If we are ever tempted to forget the difference between Miguel de Cervantes' times and our own, we are reminded here how remote his times were from ours. Nowadays there is no writer, no matter how insignificant, who would publicly admit that anybody's work was better than his own, because he honestly regarded it as superior to any other work, past or present. Nowadays there is nobody who knocks away the pedestal of his own fame. On the contrary, everybody takes the utmost care of it, and entrusts the business of building it up to no hands but his own, because no others can make it fine enough to suit him.

At this time Cervantes came into closer and more constant touch with actors and theatre managers. He had brought a few drafts of plays with him from Algiers. He completed them, and offered them to the best known managers of the playhouses in the capital : Villegas, Rios, Alonso de Morales, Sayavedra (with a patronymic so similar to that which Miguel later adopted as his own), and, especially Jerónimo Velázquez and Tomás Gutiérrez, the most famous of them all, with whom he became on terms of close friendship.

All the plays of his early period such as *Numantia* and *The Usages of Algiers*, which have come down to us, and *The Great Turquoise*, *The Naval Battle*, *Jerusalem*, *The Gallant Arsinda*, and *The Treaty of Constantinople*, which have been lost, were staged " without anybody throwing cucumbers or anything else," as he puts it himself.

But the probable pleasures of his honeymoon with fame, and the less probable ones of his honeymoon with his wife, ended with a painful loss. For old Rodrigo de Cervantes, his father, came the time of his rest after all the troubles of his life.

Rodrigo had found no repose in his random roaming along the roads of Castile or in the damp, narrow streets of its towns. He had found no peace of mind, first with the worry of providing for his family, and then with the grief of knowing that his sons were in slavery, which he felt as much in his heart as though he were suffering it in his own person. He had to come to his last hour before he reached the rest for which he longed.

He died in the middle of the year 1785, with such fortitude of mind that, almost at his last moment, " he took his will in his hands and read it, and, after reading it, said that so he stipulated." Even in his choice of the place where he was to rest eternally his thoughts were fixed on the sons for whose sakes he had suffered so much. He ordered that he should be buried in the Order of Mercy monastery, so that he might be beside those who had ransomed his son Rodrigo.

Miguel felt the pain of his father's death so deeply, so intimately, that, little by little, he abandoned the friendship and the company of actors, and shut himself up at home to enjoy what love might remain to him there. But his wife did not understand him, and Miguel found more comfort in the house of his sister Magdalena, with whom his mother lived, and in that of his other sister Andrea.

His playwrighting had proved a pleasant pastime rather than a source of livelihood. He abandoned it altogether at this time, severed his relations with the players, and turned in other directions to seek his daily bread.

The public had received his productions with indifference, if not, as he says, with active hostility. The laxity of the strolling player's life became distasteful to him, in these days when his heart was in mourning for his father and for his own love, less fortunate than he had dreamed.

But, above all, he turned from playwrighting because in those days, as in ours, the stage was a labyrinth in which the best intentions got lost in the dead-ends of actors' stupidity, and the highest genius was stultified by intrigues due to rivalry and jealousy. Miguel, used though he was to fighting against adversity, did not feel strong enough to strive against backbiting and meanness. He withdrew, beaten by disgust and disappointment.

" I laid down my pen," he says, with infinite bitterness in his words, " and abandoned playwrighting. I had other things with which to concern myself. . . ."

CHAPTER XVI

So he left the steps in front of the church of San Felipe the Royal, that gossip-centre of Madrid, laboratory of rumour and clearing-house of news, which reached there by all the roads of Spain and set off again in the opposite direction, carried by courier and word of mouth.

There he must have met some of the disciples of López de Hoyos, with whom he had been friends in earlier days. There he gossiped with fops and bullies, with penniless poets and writers of satirical verse, mercenaries of anybody who had a wrong to avenge or an insult to repay, but did not dare to hire a bravo.

There he returned the daring glance of a veiled woman with a smile, and bared his head at the passage of a royal officer or a Papal preacher, with the same politeness and humility as he had once done before Don John of Lepanto or in the presence of his colonel, Don Lope.

But now he was far away from the playhouses where his very modest triumphs had been staged, and from the wretched streets of the Huertas and Cantarranas districts, where all the would-be geniuses of the period lodged. Now he was on his way to Andalusia, which had enchanted his eyes and all his senses during the years of his adolescence.

His sisters and his mother remained in Madrid. His wife returned to Esquivias, not grieving much over the departure of her husband. Henceforth she was to see him only at long intervals and then only for a few days, until, years later, old age, trouble and death reunited them.

At the end of the year 1585 Cervantes went to Seville on some business or other. It was soon after this that he hung up his pen, so high that he could not reach it again until his great mind raised him up to write *Don Quixote*.

All the following year he spent in making petitions and kicking his heels in ante-rooms, humbler than ever now in the patience with which he waited and the modesty of his demands; for, after all his trials and troubles, and his discovery that his gift for poetry earned him more appreciation than reward, his hopes and his desires alike had been whittled away.

Then officials were wanted to tour Andalusia and collect provisions from its impoverished villages for the supply of the Armada which Philip II was dispatching against Elizabeth of England. At the end of the year 1586, Miguel obtained an appointment as one of these commissioners. At the beginning of the next year he set off for Seville, that "refuge of the rejected," as he once called it, doubtless because all those who were not Fortune's favourites drifted there.

We cannot be sure at whose hands he received this appointment, but it was probably at those of Don Antonio de Guevara, Purveyor-General of the Fleet. In Seville he was to place himself under the orders of Don Diego de Valvidia, judge of the High Court of Seville, who was taking Don Antonio's place in his absence. There he met his old friend the theatre manager Tomás Gutiérrez, who had exchanged the stage for innkeeping, and now kept, in Seville, the cleanest and best found hostelry in the whole city. An old poem which deals with inns has this to say about Tomás Gutiérrez's:

" Now firstly when you come
To that good inn
In the street of Bayonne
Where princes lodge,
They give you a clean room
Up high, and a good bed,
All hung with tapestry;
And in winter a room down low
Cosy with taffetas
And damasks. Silver
Is the table ware:
Cruet, pitcher and goblet."

Here Miguel took up his lodging, rather because of the ex-theatre manager's liking for the poet than because the poor commissioner was in any position to pay the ordinary tariff at this inn where princes lodged and the table ware was of silver. He had reason to be grateful to the good Tomás, not only for giving him board and lodging for very little money, but also for providing him with a first-class view of the world. At this time the inn in the Calle de Bayona was an open book, in which every day a page was written wherein life was to be studied letter by letter.

Here came those who were setting off for the Indies, in quest of fame and fortune, or seeking forgetfulness: the former with their eyes wide open to stare at the new path which unfolded before their eyes; the latter with eyes downcast, so that they should not see even memory. Here came those returning from overseas; most of them ruined and broken, whose sole desire was to keep their eyes closed, so that before them might rise the images which had charmed their far-off, better years; but a few of them prosperous, ostentatious, and proud in their belief that Fortune had yielded them her fruits by dint of their merits, rather than by caprice of her own fickle will.

Along the Calle de Bayona passed men coming from the brothel district near by: bravoes and ruffians, veterans of Flanders and Italy, carriers and porters. Sometimes the retinue of a prince drew rein at the inn.

In the pleadings in the quaint lawsuit which Tomás Gutiérrez took against the Confraternity of the Most Holy Sacrament of El Sagrario, because it refused to admit him as a member, on the ground that he had been a play-actor, there are passages of juicy reading which show us what Sevillian life was like at that time. In others the innkeeper, in his defence of the profession of play-actor, gives proof of wit and learning.

"It is true," he says in his attestation, "that I was an actor when I was young and homeless, away from my native town and my family; but this is not a menial profession, but one calling for much cleverness and skill, which has its origin in the patriarchs, the kings and the prophets and the Roman Curia."

Then he defends himself against the imputation of being a mere innkeeper, and presents himself as a man of substance who keeps a leading house, fit and proper for the entertainment of grandees.

"It is not true that I am an innkeeper. I have one of the most important houses in the Calle de Bayona, opposite the *gradas* of this city, for which I pay Don Diego Mexias de la Ruelas three hundred ducats a year, and in it I receive and serve the Duke of Alba and the Duke of Osuna, the Marquis of Priego, the Duke of Francavilla, the Marquis of Villanueva, the Duke of Segorbe, Don Luis de Haro, son of Don Diego de Haro and brother of the Marquis of Carpio;

the Marquis of La Yatara, judges of Rome and of the Nuncio, the judge of the galleys of Spain, justices of the *mesta* (cattle breeders' guild), generals and colonels, judges, inquisitors and justices of the King, and other grandees of Spain, who, because there is no other house and lodging in this city more respected and convenient, come and stay in it, which is a matter of public knowledge, as is also the fact that I have in my house men slaves and women slaves to wait upon them, good beds and very good treatment at my hands, and in wrought silver and furniture in my house I have the value of six thousand ducats; and this treatment of mine is very highly esteemed in Italy and France; and in Madrid and Valladolid, though with less expense than here, very influential men and respected gentlemen carry on the same business; and a distinction must be drawn between me and innkeepers who receive muleteers in their houses and take the packsaddles off their beasts and wash their sores. . . ."

Such was the distinguished company with which Cervantes associated during his stays in Seville, on his return from the villages where he had gone to collect his spoils of wheat and oil.

He had a very small room in the attics, with a pine table. At this table he drew up his accounts of collection. At it he kept on writing prose and verse with just as true a ring, just as finely worked and highly polished, as the silver goblets out of which Alba and Haro drank sherry in this inn of Tomás Gutiérrez's.

But such hours were the briefest in this new life of Cervantes. Most of his time he spent riding the rough roads which led from Seville to Castro del Rio, to Espejo, to La Rambla and to Ecija, where he had to discharge his wearisome duties as commissioner, on the back of a lean and sorry nag: the sire, at least in imagination, of the steed which was later to be the comrade, rather than the servant, of the Ingenuous Knight.

With him went his constable and assistant, who served as his guard of honour on the roads and as his second in putting the screw on to make the wretched peasants produce the provisions which were to pass into the hands of purveyors and their deputies. There a good deal of them stuck, like fine dust of a process which, indeed, was one of grinding.

The purveyor to the galleys decided what every village ought to provide in the way of wheat and oil. The village councillors countered with a complaint that they would find it difficult to get together the quantity required. They supported their request for its reduction by pointing to the record of other recent imposts and recalling the bad harvest and the poverty of the place—for all places were poor in these days of glorious wretchedness.

When agreement on the quantity had been reached, the mayor was advised of the impending arrival of the commissioner. Even then, the envoy did not find the provisions ready for him. Nor did he find the peasants any too eager to hand them over. They wanted to keep their supplies for the maintenance of their families and as seed for their arable land.

The subjects of His Majesty were not required to provide this wheat and oil for the Armada as a tribute to the King. The commodities were handed over in return for a receipt, by virtue of which they would be paid for as soon as there was any money with which to pay for them. But the position of the treasury was too embarrassed for anybody to be able to put much confidence in its credit, and the commissioner finally left the place taking the people's hatred with him along with their wheat.

117

The commissioner was aware of the hostility which awaited him on his arrival and would speed him on his way. Nevertheless, he had to have a heavy hand and harden his heart against sobs and sighs; for the purveyor, his chief, urged him on like a greyhound after his prey, dangling before him the bait of a wretched salary which he would lose if he did not know his business. The result was that the commissioner closed his ears to all complaints, took by main force what he could not get by good will, broke into houses, and put anybody who offered resistance to him by word or act into prison.

Among the commissioners, as in all other professions, were to be found men of all kinds. There were some who added insult to exaction, and, in addition to what was required for the King, took whatever they thought fit for themselves. There were others who regretted the wretchedness they brought in their train. If they lent themselves to this office, it was because they were driven by necessity, and because they knew that, if they refused it, there were plenty to take their places, without any advantage to the unfortunate peasants.

Among the former class were those to whom Philip II referred in his royal decree:

"... the harm and extortion which the commissioners and constables of the purveyors habitually practise against the vassals and peasants of Andalusia, over and above the collection of the wheat, barley and other supplies required for the provision; for which no remedy has yet been found, in spite of the close supervision and exemplary punishment that have been employed."

Among the latter class was to be numbered Miguel, large-hearted and broad-minded, as he showed on many

118

occasions, who was driven to this wretched profession only through misfortune.

When Cervantes arrived at Ecija on his business of seeking provision for the needs of the fleet, the town was still bemoaning the last, and very rigorous, exaction which it had undergone. The orders of the King were that victuals were not to be taken except in return for good money; but the King confined himself to issuing these orders without producing the necessary gold, and the commissioners found themselves, once more, under the painful necessity of disobeying His Majesty to the greater glory of his armed forces.

Ecija did not receive the news of the fresh exaction with any good will. It was in face of the hostility of the town that Commissioner Cervantes had to seek, attach, collect and warehouse his supplies.

Among the lots which he took were some which belonged to the parish of Santa Cruz, to the Dean and Chapter of Seville, and to the seminary of the same cathedral.

Cervantes was astonished to receive the smack in the face with which the Church replied to his daring. The vicar of Ecija and the chapter of Seville thundered censure and excommunication against him. Miguel was not as yet aware of the fact that the property with which clerics and canons ministered to their needs was of Divine origin, and that it was sacrilege for any commissioner to lay his impious hands upon it.

This was the first of the many traps into which Cervantes stumbled in his office as tax-gatherer, and he had to wrestle with his conscience and stifle it before he could get ecclesiastical authority to clear him of censure and ex-communication.

Years later, in a page of his immortal book, he was to sum up in a few ironical words his troubles and tremors of those days:

" We have run up against the Church, Sancho."

CHAPTER XVII

CERVANTES did not take warning from this mishap. It affected merely his conscience, and that could scarcely tutor him when his job itself was at stake.

In January of the next year, he was back once more at Ecija, with a fresh commission from the same purveyor Guevara. The people of Ecija lodged protests in quarters where they thought their lamentations were likely to be heard; but the authorities neither of Heaven nor of earth listened to them, for the Marquis of Santa Cruz was calling for supplies with which to feed the soldiers and sailors who were concentrating at the port of Lisbon.

All through the early part of this year, and more and more insistently, the fleet demanded supplies. When the Marquis of Santa Cruz fell seriously ill and the Duke of Medina Sidonia took over the command, the new admiral, who scarcely knew starboard from port, concerned himself about nothing but his rheumatism and the provisioning of the ships with " salt meat, pork and salted codfish, as well as bread-stuffs."

First from Lisbon, and then from Corunna, where the first of the storms which assailed the " Invincible " Armada drove it, he wrote to the King with complaints about the state of his supplies. " In consequence of the provisions having been on board so long, they have gone so bad, putrid and unusable that I find myself in great difficulties about feeding my men, and am in no position to improve matters. . . . What we particularly need is meat and fish, for of these we are notably short, and other supplies are required as well."

Though historians have made fun of his memory, Medina Sidonia was a good commander at least in this respect: that, in the case of things which he understood, such as cheese and salted cod, he showed himself far-seeing and scrupulously conscientious. Where he failed was in knowledge of naval matters, and to his ignorance of them has been attributed the disaster which, a few months later, scattered the armada off the coasts of Great Britain.

But it would be fairer to blame the King who believed that to be born a member of the illustrious Guzman family, and to have been a master of equestrian exercises and bullfighting in his youth, sufficed to make a man informed about all things in connection with earth, sea and sky, like Vishnu. So Philip appointed Medina Sidonia to the command of the " Invincible " Armada. Equestrian exercises, however, and the gift of being well dressed and well spoken, have very little relation with the command of a fleet. The Duke himself, on his appointment, informed Philip how ill fitted he was for the command, inasmuch as " his state of health was not suited to seafaring, since from his little experience of it he suffered from sea-sickness, and he was also very rheumatic."

The admiral's requests were transmitted through Madrid to the purveyors in Andalusia, and Miguel went from place to place, sowing hatred of himself in order to reap good wheat.

In Castro del Rio he came into collision with the Church again. By order of his chief, the purveyor Guevara, no distinction was to be made in this emergency between clergy and laity. " Wherever he discovers that the said wheat and barley are to be found, and to whatever quantity he may discover, he shall take possession of them from whatever person may hold them, of whatever estate and condition he may be, ecclesiastic or layman." Then are set forth the penalties which will be incurred by any person who resists this order, promulgated for " the greater convenience and benefit of His Majesty's Royal Treasury."

But the sacristan of Castro del Rio opposed the requisitioning by the commissioner of a small quantity of wheat which was the property of the Church. Cervantes found himself compelled to put this rebellious subject in prison; and, in consequence, a second anathema was launched against him. The Vicar-general of Cordoba excommunicated him, and ordered his name to be inscribed on the black list at the door of the church.

It was no excuse for Cervantes that he was simply the executant of an order of the purveyor to the royal galleys. It was not enough that this order said with absolute clarity: " ecclesiastic or layman." Perhaps the Vicar-general of the diocese held that lay authority had no jurisdiction over his wheat. Or perhaps he did not consider that the person of the sacristan was expressly covered in Antonio de Guevara's authorisation by the clause which I have quoted, inasmuch as, being a sacristan, he was not a cleric, though neither could he be called a layman. It would have been better, for Cervantes' ease of conscience, if the order had been more specific and covered " ecclesiastics, laymen and sacristans."

In any case, the sense of responsibility which was apparent in Miguel's bearing, and the obvious sincerity of his winning ways, gradually secured him the confidence and liking of

123

other people. So much was this so that, when it became known that the purveyor Guevara was now in a position to redeem the credit notes which he had issued, everybody handed over to Cervantes the receipts which attested the treasury's debt and entrusted him with bringing back the money.

This fact, and the vindication of him which was forthcoming from the municipal council of Ecija, when the local magistrate was ordered by royal decree to "investigate the taking of a certain quantity of barley from this town by the commissioners"—a decree between whose lines could be read a suspicion of malversation—constitute the clearest proof that Cervantes kept his good name in his exercise of this office, when only too many of his colleagues succumbed to the temptation of easy pilfering to augment their exiguous pay, quieting their consciences by saying that it was quite legitimate to defraud such a remote and immaterial entity as the State.

In their report, the municipal councillors of Ecija declared that Cervantes had gone about his business of requisitioning wheat "with the utmost rectitude"; that they had never heard that he had "done anything improper"; and that hitherto he had "done his duty as commissioner well and faithfully."

In the performance of this duty Cervantes spent the greater part of his time, which he might have employed more fruitfully for himself, and for us, if some Divine decree had entrusted him with duties which would have brought him in more money.

When he had a day or two of leisure, he went back to his inn in the Calle de Bayona in Seville, that resting-place of princes. Never had it a better right to boast this title than when it sheltered Cervantes, that prince among geniuses.

But most of his days he passed on the road, talking to the muleteers who drove their string of pack animals, laden with the hides of Cordoba, the wine of La Mancha, the oil of Jaen, or the fruit of Murcia, when it was in season; or to country priests and the provincial priestlings, let loose from the seminaries and universities with their dog Latin, who were now scouring the roads to carry salvation to men, relying on Divine Goodness rather than on any settled income.

It must have been during one of his stays in Seville, or in the course of some scabrous conversation with some carrier or other wayfarer, that Miguel heard about the disaster to the Spanish Armada. It may have been when he went back to Seville from Ecija, with his quantum of one thousand five hundred *arrobas* of oil, for whose collection Guevara commended him on 20th October; or some days before, when he set off from Seville for Ecija to supervise the transport of two thousand *fanegas* of wheat for milling.

Some talkative cleric, on his Castilian mule, may have stopped him and told him the bad news. The King had ordered the cessation of the prayers and penances through whose medium God had been petitioned for the triumph of the Spanish Armada, since it was no longer requisite to seek Divine aid, but rather to give thanks to God that the disaster to the Armada had been no greater.

" Events at sea," said the resigned monarch in his letter to the bishops,

" have been of divers kinds, as is now known and as the commander of the Armada has reported. You may already have heard that the

Duke of Medina Sidonia has arrived with part of it at the port of Santander, and other ships have arrived elsewhere, some of them damaged after the long and difficult voyage they have made. Inasmuch as we owe God thanks for all that He is pleased to do, I have given Him thanks for this, and for the clemency He has shown us all; for, in view of the unfavourable weather and the danger in which the whole Armada found itself from the wild and furious storm it encountered, we might with good reason have feared a worse event, and that we have been spared this I attribute to the prayers and supplications which were offered with such devotion."

The Spanish sovereign may have been very thankful to Heaven that there had been " no worse event." He should have been even more thankful for the quiet resignation with which he was able to bear the news that ninety ships, with eight thousand men, had been sunk through his own fault.

But perhaps Cervantes, less disposed to resignation, except in the case of his own troubles, shook his fist towards the northern sky, under whose mists sheltered those enemies of his faith and fatherland, more abhorred now that those other enemies who infested the " Inner Sea " with their corsair ships. Through his mind must have passed the memory of those hours of Lepanto, full of bloodshed and feverish enthusiasm. He must have remembered the youthful figure of Don John, who fell into his brother's disfavour because he wanted, upstart chick that he was, to fly alongside the Spanish Eagle.

" Very differently would things have gone with the ' Invincible ' Armada, in spite of all the elements being unleashed against it, if it had been in the hands of Don John," Miguel doubtless reflected, as the talkative priest, or whoever it was that sententiously imparted his information, told him the news from Madrid.

126

Miguel must have felt a great depression descend upon him from the autumnal sky streaked with gusty clouds, and exhale towards him from the fields where the yellow spikes of stubble still stood erect. He must have thought of all those who, like Don John, felt within them the capacity for great deeds, but found jealousy lying in ambush for them, ready to spring upon them, muffle them in a cloak of silence and oblivion, and kill them little by little with bitter draughts of disappointment. All kinds of sad ideas stirred in his mind, just as the dead leaves rustled on the hard road under his horse's hoofs. . . .

CHAPTER XVIII

SINCE the glory of Castile was a monster insatiable for blood, gold and provisions, in spite of the rout of the Armada the king continued, through the agency of the purveyors and their commissioners, to lay hands on other people's property. It was still much against their will, for they were not satisfied even if they were paid for it. They counted on making more if they sold in a free market; and, if they required supplies for their own use, they had to pay more than they received from the king.

In February of the year 1589, Miguel made a sworn report of his expenditure in connection with the milling of flour at Ecija.

> "All which I swear by God and by the sign of the Cross that I spent in payment of the mill, and in many other expenses which I do not enumerate, and I sign this with my name, this sixth of February of 1589."

After carrying out other commissions on behalf of the purveyor *ad interim*, Miguel de Oviedo, and presenting further sworn statements of his expenses in connection with them, Cervantes wearied of his vexatious job as a commissioner.

Under date 21st May 1590, he sent a petition to the president of the Council of the Indies. In this petition, after setting forth the services and the captivity of himself and his brother Rodrigo, he begged that he might be made "beneficiary of one of the offices in the Indies out of the

three or four at present vacant, either the paymastership
of the kingdom of New Granada, or the governorship of
the province of Soconusco in Guatemala, or the paymastership of the galleys at Cartagena, or the magistracy in
the city of La Paz."

But his modest request received no more reply than
what was customary, whenever it was a matter of getting
rid of some importunate poor fellow who murmured his
prayers and supplications outside a closed door. The " Some
other time, brother," with which you refuse a beggar
assumed more conventional form under the pen of some
clerk in the office of the Council of the Indies, and the
answer came back to Miguel expressed in more polite
language ; but it conveyed the same far-off promise, the
same deceptive hope : " Try somewhere else."

There are commentators on the life of Cervantes, like the
good León Mainez, who raise hands trembling with indignation to Heaven, demanding posthumous punishment upon
all those who failed to appreciate, and to reward, all the
genius, all the worth, all the virtue assembled in his person.
" We are overcome with indignation when we observe
their behaviour, when we note their indifference, when we
consider their injustice."

Blessed, say I, be those who had no eyes to see, because,
in their blindness, they were midwives of the good knight
of La Mancha, who might never have come into this world
if my lords of the Council of the Indies had sent the
author of his days overseas. Even if we do not bear this
in mind, we may still forgive them, instead of clamour-
ing to Heaven in passionate phrases for their eternal
damnation.

I   129

Too many were the maimed, too many were the crippled, too many were those who had suffered captivity and wretchedness for the glory of Spain and Don Philip, for all of them to be tended and have their hurts salved with appointments and rewards. Miguel did not bear on his brow, like another Moses, a horn of light to show that he was one of God's elect.

The only one of his works which had as yet been published was his *Galatea*. It had been well received by the public; but it had not got so far as to penetrate into the offices of Ministers of the Crown or the royal apartments, both of them places where the air was stale and the light came in dimmed by dusty windows. *Galatea* was fresh air and sunlight, good only for reading beneath the pines in the mountains or on the flowery banks of some river.

Miguel did not get what he wanted. Perhaps these days from towards the end of 1589 until the date of his petition were the bitterest and the most aimless of his life. He had come to hate the job to which he had been driven by sheer necessity. Not only was it unattractive to him; he also felt that it was insecure, at the mercy of the whim of the purveyors, who might at any moment dispense with his services.

As he had done once before, he scanned all paths, uncertain which one he should choose in life. But then he had been in the years of his youth, when all casements open on a sea without shores, across which the ship of hope may voyage where she will. Now he bore the burden of bitterness, of disappointment, and of approaching old age, and the horizon was closing in upon him.

He tried to take the path to the Indies because it ran farthest, and along it hope would last longest; for by now he was so poor in hopes that he caressed the last of them and clasped it lovingly to his breast, just like a beggar who suddenly finds a piece of gold in his hand.

By this time he had left Tomás Gutiérrez's inn, because he would not live, more comfortably than his means permitted, on charity. The generous innkeeper let him off all he owed, in return for a certain bad debt which Miguel made over to him.

To live in a way more suited to his condition, Miguel took a " residential house in the district of La Magdalena," which was rented in the name of one Jerónima Alarcón. This name, like many other names, flits across Cervantes' life, like a fragment of paper borne by the wind which falls on to a bonfire, flares for a moment, and disappears, without our knowing anything else about it. Jerónima Alarcón was doubtless the heroine of another humble and obscure love affair, like his affair in Naples or his affair with Anna Rojas.

Meanwhile his legitimate love—that love which was really more fugitive than those which chance put in his way—was all alone at Esquivias, forgetful of Miguel. She knew nothing about his trials and troubles in the towns of Andalusia and his straitened circumstances in Seville; or, if she did know, she heaved the gentlest of sighs over them, just as you do over something that has happened in some far-off country to people you do not know.

After presenting his petition to the Council of the Indies, but before he had received their lordships' reply, Miguel granted a power of attorney to his wife and to his sister Magdalena, authorising them, in his absence, to deal with any of his affairs as they thought fit. We can gather from this that he hoped for a favourable reply to his petition, and wanted to put his affairs in Spain in good order in readiness for his departure for America.

Meanwhile, he returned to his lifelong taste for letters, and lamented the disaster to the Armada in passionate verses, through which flits a memory of the wretched consolation invented by the King.

> " Does it not cut you to the heart,
>   O Spain, our mother,
>   To see your sons returning to your breast
>   Leaving the sea strewn with their wrack;
>   Even though 'twas not the foeman's might
>   That turned them back, but storm invincible
>   Of all the elements that helped the foe
>   To dare to show his head? "

At this time a literary *salon* existed in Seville, a kind of free academy, presided over by Don Francisco Pacheco, who was distinguished both as painter and as poet. Perhaps his greatest glory was that he received into his family, by giving him his daughter for wife, that prodigy of art, the great Don Diego de Velázquez. Don Francisco Pacheco kept open house for " all men of talent, both Sevillians and strangers," so Rodrigo Caro tells us in his *Famous Men*. In competition with the painter-poet, the Duke of Alcalá and Don Juan de Arguijo also threw their lordly homes open to the prose and verse writers of the period.

Miguel de Cervantes, as a visiting bard, may perhaps have

frequented some of the " academies," but there is no proof, as some of his biographers claim, that he was a friend of Pacheco's. The painter's famous *Book of Portraits*, in which all those who attended his " academy " figure, does not contain any portrait of Cervantes; nor, in his *Journey to Parnassus*, does Cervantes refer to Pacheco. At the same time, in this poem he sings the praises of other poets whose names would never have come down to us if such illustrious hands as his had not taken the trouble to pass them down the centuries.

In his *Journey to Parnassus*, Cervantes lauds all, or almost all, the painter's friends, such as Ochoa, Herrera, and Arguijo. But, because he was familiar with the work of these distinguished poets and delighted in singing their praises, it does not follow that he was on friendly terms with them. Pacheco himself, the author of a didactic poem about painting, may have been quite unknown to Cervantes both as a poet and as a man.

If he did not take advantage of his enforced leisure as a commissioner, and of any leisure he allowed himself as a writer, to frequent the literary gatherings of his time, he must have made better use of it in getting to know mankind. He frequented the meeting-places of bravoes and busybodies, even though there he might not find occasion to study mankind in its highest forms. So he made the acquaintance of queer old men of false respectability, loose old women, wenches of easy virtue, the Chiquiznaques and Maniferros: all that company of the Court of Miracles in the courtyard of Monipodio, which he presents to us in the most finished gem of that shining string of jewels, his *Exemplary Tales*.

There is a passage in one of them that reveals to us very clearly an addiction of Miguel's, which was common and in no way censured at that time, nor censurable at any other time. He was an admirer of nuns.

"Isabella's parents," he tells us in this work,

> "rented a large house opposite Santa Paula's, because there was in that convent a nun who was a cousin of hers, whose voice was unique in its exquisiteness. . . . And to identify her it was not necessary to do any more than ask for the nun who had the best voice in the convent."

Miguel was in the habit of scattering his own enthusiasms about his writings. Doubtless he spent many an hour listening to the voice of this girl whom he was never to meet, but with whom, nevertheless, he fell in love. He would go to the convent church at the hour of Vespers, when the dimness of the church lent itself to his shy longing. The choir was lit only by a chandelier far overhead, which bathed it in a soft, melancholy light. Through the lattice could be discerned the figures of the nuns, and among them was she who had borrowed the voice of an angel to charm poor human beings. It filled them with overflowing tenderness, and they wept as they listened to her.

Cervantes was not so much in love with a nun as in love with an ideal, like his own Don Alonso the Good. His forty years, spent in a life of privation and disappointment, did not now permit him to play the part of a beau and a gallant. He could not even dress the part. He was reduced by this time to clothing himself in coarse mixed cloth, and even that obtained on credit.

He spent many an hour with his eyes fixed on the light

that filtered through the cross-bars of the lattice, watching the figures of the nuns and asking himself, with anxious tenderness, which of them was the girl who had " the best voice in the Santa Paula convent."

The times were very different from our own, and, despite the strictness which Saint Theresa and Saint John of the Cross sought to introduce into monasteries and convents, there were few young nuns without an admirer who plied them with compliments and presents of ribbons and hand-kerchiefs. Some of the nuns were even given facilities for meeting their admirers, as we learn, among other sources, from that clever humorist and agreeable narrator of his perambulations about the by-ways of Valladolid, then the capital of the Spains, the Portuguese gentleman Tomé Pinheiro da Veiga:

" My friends got on better with the nuns," he says on one occasion, " *who, as such, entertained them as wittily as they could.*"

Further on, describing a party given by the nuns of a certain convent, he adds:

" The Devil, who is always lurking behind the door to trip up anybody who gives him a chance and get his claws into him, led me to a spot where I should have stumbled if I had not held on tight; for, looking about me, I found that I was beside a young nun, with lovely green eyes, very calm and modest: the kind of eyes that Camoens calls tired, but not of killing; a girl grave and discreet, with a modest smile and a smiling modesty. . . .

" And, when I noticed her raising her eyes again, I paid her a compliment, though a mild one, which she received with a sweetness that made my heart leap. . . . She knew what perturbation she was causing me, and she recompensed me with a compassion which, in other circumstances, would have clad me in the livery of hope. . . ."

135

Our gentleman of Alcalcá was not so lucky, or so closely tempted, as the Portuguese gentleman. He had to content himself, in default of " lovely green eyes," with listening to a melodious voice which was the consolation of his sad hours.

CHAPTER XIX

WHEN Guevara retired from the purveyorship, his place was taken by the Basque, Pedro de Isunza, who entrusted Cervantes with the same powers as he had received from his predecessor.

Accordingly Miguel returned to his peregrinations about the Andalusian countryside. But the itch to write troubled him either through the mere working of his genius, or through contagion, if it be a fact that at this time he came into contact in the " academies " of Seville with persons suffering from the same disease.

He chanced to meet Rodrigo Osorio, a well-known theatre manager, with whom he had been friends when the two of them were in Madrid. A long talk with the manager left Cervantes rejuvenated in his belief in his writing powers, and he undertook on the spot to send Osorio half a dozen plays, as they were written, at the price of fifty ducats apiece. But so sure of his inspiration was he that he added that he would forgo his right to payment if, when one of his plays was staged, " it appears that it is not one of the best in all Spain."

A few days after this conversation, which ended with such high hopes, Miguel had his first encounter with the law and its officers. It was a more serious matter than his brushes with the Church, because he could forget her anathemas and dispose of them, like importunate thoughts, by the simple process of passing his hand across his brow.

But constables and officers of the law seized him so firmly, body and mind, that never again was he to be very far from their clutches. When he was free in body, he found himself harried by endless, insistent demands for presentation of his accounts, which pursued him all through his days, until finally, now worn thin and sharp as arrows, they stuck themselves into his old age, like some new disease of it.

It was in the course of 1592 that the magistrate of Ecija who had jurisdiction over commissioners, Francisco Moscoso, ordered Miguel's arrest at Castro del Rio, where he was at the moment, on a charge of having taken possession of three hundred *fanegas* of wheat from the public granary of Ecija and sold them without authority to do so. That was the end for the time being of his idea of returning to the Muses. Osorio the theatre manager was left without his plays, and Miguel was left without his ducats.

He had his hands full with the hard job of defending himself against this unjust accusation. Valid though his defence might be, it did not do him much good; for he found himself sentenced by this magistrate Moscoso to repay the value of the three hundred *fanegas* of wheat, at the rate of fourteen reales the *fanega*. In addition, he was fined six thousand maravedies towards war expenses, and had to pay costs to the extent of four days' salary and legal and travelling expenses of the magistrate and his officers.

He was released under bond that he could raise this money. But he was released only to experience another, and a greater, misfortune: that of finding his patron, Don Pedro de Isunza, caught in the same meshes in which he had become entangled.

During the previous year, 1591, a commissioner of Isunza's and a colleague of Miguel's, by name Nicolas Benito, had visited the town of Teba. He encountered resistance in removing the grain from its granaries, and accordingly forced their doors and took possession of rather more than one thousand *fanegas* of wheat and five hundred of barley.

He was prosecuted for this proceeding by a magistrate named Fresnada, who, in the existing confusion of jurisdictions, believed that Nicolas Benito's action came within the scope of his own. Fresnada brought the same charge against Benito as his colleague Moscoso did against Cervantes. Neither of them was backward in inflicting fines and costs and requiring bail, though the innocence of both the accused was subsequently proved.

But Fresnada, more wily than Moscoso, regarded Nicolas Benito as a mere nobody who was scarcely likely to yield any gold dust which the hands that squeezed him might pocket. He turned his fire against Benito's principal, the purveyor Isunza, a man of wealth and substance.

Proceedings were taken against Isunza. He was called upon to justify, or to indemnify, the acts of violence committed by his subordinates on these and other occasions; for it was hoped to widen the scope of the trial and turn it into an easily worked gold-mine.

Miguel had been referred to, incidentally, in the course of Isunza's trial as one of the purveyor's servants and mandatories; and, before his own arrest, he had offered some evidence, of no great importance—doubtless because, at this point, the trial had not yet taken the bad turn which was later to be given it by clever lawyers. On his release, however, Miguel, seeing how badly matters were now going for Isunza, betook himself to Madrid and spontaneously presented a statement to His Majesty, dated 1st December, in defence of his patron in disgrace.

Once more, amid the wretched environment in which he found himself—commissioners, tax-gatherers, magistrates, lawyers and constables—there emerged the Miguel de Cervantes of his heroic days in Algiers. It was only a flash, a fugitive cut-back to those days; but a flash it was, swift, stark, pristine and pure as lightning itself.

Once more, on behalf of a friend, Miguel was risking, not, this time, his life—for now it was such a poor thing that it was not worth while taking it from him, nor was it worth his offering to lose it—but something that he held in even greater esteem: his good name and reputation.

Unasked by anybody, he flung his own honour into the sea of this trial, so that it should swim to the help of his drowning friend, heedless that it might itself sink to the bottom if his attempt at rescue failed.

" It is not right that such things as are charged against us should be said about the said purveyor or myself," he declares in his testimony, " or that the said purveyor should be unjustly treated.

> " And in order that this truth may be made manifest, I offer to give evidence in this court, or wherever else Your Majesty may decide, and also to give bail, bond and security for him, over and above what I have already given to the said purveyor, to pay any sums which he may be sentenced to pay; and may it please Your Majesty that, in view of this bail of mine, and of the evidence which I am prepared to offer, the said purveyor and his possessions be not molested, *inasmuch as he is guiltless*."

No notice was taken of this petition of Miguel's; nor did it, like his self-sacrifice in Algiers, avail anything beyond drawing the ill-will of the high and mighty down upon himself.

Pedro de Isunza, ill and embittered, retired to Puerto de Santa Maria, where, a little later, in June of the following year, he surrendered his soul to God. Miguel surrendered, if not his soul, at least his peace of mind into lower hands; for in the year 1598 we still find him involved in the charges and findings of Isunza's trial.

After Isunza's death, the duties of purveyor were again entrusted to the man who had discharged them before Guevara, Miguel de Oviedo. The new purveyor knew Cervantes and trusted him, and so he kept him in his employment.

Under the orders of this new patron of his, Miguel toured the villages of Paterna, Niebla, Almonte, Rociana, Bolullos, Palma, and other places in the neighbourhood of Huelva.

It was during this tour of his that he received from Madrid the saddest news that could possibly reach him. In a wretched house in the Calle de Leganitos, in the early days of November, 1593, death had come to his mother, Doña Leonor de Cortinas, that poor old woman who had so often forgotten her own sorrows and remembered nothing but her sons' sorrows in their captivity, or in their freedom to follow paths that led only to poverty and misfortune.

When he heard this news, Miguel decided to return to the capital to see the surviving members of his family again, and in the spring of 1594 he set off for Madrid.

Shortly before this, orders had been issued that the system of collecting supplies in the province of Andalusia was to be reorganised. Miguel was afraid of finding himself once more without employment.

He called upon some of his friends, and, having obtained

141

their support, applied on 1st July for a post equivalent to his now lost job of commissioner. As his guarantor he offered Francisco Suárez Gascó, resident in Tarancon, and, as sureties for Suárez's solvency, the accountant Agustín de Cetina, Don Gabriel Suárez and Juan Valera, all residents in Madrid. As even all this did not appear sufficient to my lords of the Treasury, Cervantes, by a document executed before the notary Jerónimo Félix, on 21st August, on behalf of husband and wife, made himself answerable through the landed property and crops of his wife, Doña Catalina.

Two days later, Miguel received a commission as collector of the tax on sales and arrears of tithe in the kingdom of Granada. He was given a period of fifty days to complete his collection, at a salary of sixteen reales a day.

In spite of the fact that his commission instructed him to set out at once for the sphere of his duties, several days passed before he started. He spent the last few days of August at Esquivias with his wife, whom he had to thank for pledging her own scanty resources in order that he might be granted a means of livelihood.

They went back once more, fleetingly, to the fugitive happiness of their first love. She, still almost a girl, and he, already almost an old man, passed through the dusty streets of Esquivias, under the curious eyes of the local gossips, some of whom whispered about "the man who lost the use of his hand at Lepanto and had been a prisoner in the hands of the Moors"; while others said that it was a shame, and not like a good Christian, for a man to leave that saintly Doña Catalina deserted and forgotten.

When evening fell, the two of them went to enjoy the cool on one of the hills of the low range below which the village nestled, or to visit Doña Catalina's vineyard, with its yet unripened grapes, or her cornfields, still yellow with stubble.

From the distance came the plaintive songs of rustics and the tinkling of cattle-bells, and Miguel could feel all the peace of the plain, bathed by the setting sun, in his heart, bathed too by the setting sun of his sometime love. . . .

CHAPTER XX

CERVANTES was first instructed to collect in the province of Granada, in sales-tax, tithe and arrears, some two and a half million maravedies; but, before he set out, this sum was modified by certain rebates and additions.

He arrived at Guadix at the beginning of September, and began his collection in that town. Then he went on to Baza, where he found the business of the Treasury more involved than at Guadix. He straightened it out, and, after certain warnings to Simón Sánchez, the town steward, and Juan de Cuenca, the tax-farmer, he collected 27,904 marvedies on the principal account, plus twenty-five reales from each of them, by way of fine for their one day's delay in handing over the sums due. He also found himself compelled to punish Alonso de España, the proprietary treasurer, for the negligence and laxity with which he kept the accounts within his jurisdiction.

But when the time fixed for the completion of his mission arrived, Cervantes had not yet managed to get in all the money whose collection had been entrusted to him. On 8th October he wrote to the Treasury Council asking for an extension of time; and, as he received no reply to this letter, he wrote again on 18th November:

"... After that, I went to Vélez-Málaga; and, as the harvest had been bad, and the receivers could not collect the taxes from the tenants, I contented myself with taking bills payable on Seville. ... My time-limit has expired. May it please Your Majesty to grant me twenty days more, during which I shall have collected the whole

144

amount and I will proceed to hand over the money wherever I may be instructed. . . ."

He awaited the reply from the Council at Malaga. It was not long in coming. It granted him the extension of time he requested, but ordered him not to accept as valid the excuses for delay in payment put forward by the receiver of Almuñécar and its dependent towns of Motril and Salobreña.

"You will collect from the receivers or treasurers the said three hundred and seventy-four thousand maravedies, together with your own expenses during the time you have spent or may spend in connection with this matter, and if the treasurers and receivers do not then produce and pay the money, you will apply to them, in their persons and property, and to those of their guarantors each and all, all the executions, distraints, sales and auctions of property that may be appropriate and necessary. . . ."

On 9th December Cervantes collected his arrears in Ronda, and then, at last, those of Almuñécar, Motril and Salobreña, after which he proceeded to Seville.

Here he experienced the worst misfortune of all those which he suffered in the course of his duties as commissioner and tax-collector. Since a draft on Madrid seemed to him the simplest and least costly procedure, he handed over the sum total of his collection—some seven thousand four hundred reales—to Simón Freire, a Sevillian merchant, who gave him a bill payable in the capital. In case they should not both be there, it was to be payable by the Portuguese, Gabriel Rodríguez.

But Rodríguez did not pay it; nor did Cervantes find Freire in Madrid when he arrived in the capital, for Freire was very busy in Seville with the preliminaries to his bankruptcy.

So Simón Freire took himself off with the money he had

K   145

received from Cervantes; and, though Miguel returned to
Seville in quest of it, it was impossible to recover it, since
the merchant's property was under the control of other
creditors. Cervantes petitioned the King for an order that,
inasmuch as this money was treasury funds, it should be
credited to him, despite any liens on the property of the
bankrupt.

The King and his Ministers were ready enough to act in
their own interests. They ordered the judge Don Bernardo
de Olmedilla to proceed for the recovery of the seven
thousand reales with all possible diligence. But, as the person
and the good intentions of Miguel de Cervantes were a
matter of less importance to them, they added to the order
a paragraph which referred to him in no very friendly terms:

"... The contents of this letter, and whatever may be done in
pursuance of it, are without prejudice to the rights which I (the
King) have against the said Miguel de Cervantes and his guarantors,
who are and remain bound to discharge the said commission and
give account of it; and the said recovery of the seven thousand four
hundred reales is and remains his obligation and responsibility, and
not mine."

This unfortunate business with Freire was to persecute
Cervantes almost all his days. Seven years later, my lords of
the treasury were still uncertain what had become of all the
maravedies collected by Miguel in the kingdom of Granada.
They had to apply to the records office to clear up their
doubts by the story of the bankruptcy and the steps which
had subsequently been taken to recover the sum.

Meanwhile, Don Francisco Suárez Gascó, one of Cervantes' guarantors, was immediately called upon to answer
for the arrears. When this gentleman protested that he

neither should nor would do so until the plea of his bailie had been heard, Miguel found himself summoned to the capital again, and with no smooth words or polite requests, but under a time-limit and with the threat of prison hanging over him.

If Cervantes did not at once produce bail that within the time-limit he would present himself in Madrid and there render account of his proceedings and of the money, he was to be arrested and lodged in prison, "until the president and auditors of the said supreme auditor's office of the treasury shall otherwise decide and direct. . . ."

Miguel was in Seville, far away from anybody who would help him, and he could not find the money for the required bail. The unfortunate tax-collector might have counted on clemency and humane treatment from the good heart and the upright conscience of the judge Vallejo, who was charged with this troublesome case; but the royal orders kept the doors of the judge's generous impulses stoutly padlocked. Cervantes could not find the necessary maravedies for his bail, and the judge had no option but to order his arrest and committal to prison in accordance with the King's command.

Once more Miguel de Cervantes found himself in prison. Once more he could see the blue of evening, beneath which birds warbled and girls sang on the banks of the Guadalquivir, only through a narrow rectangle crossed by stout bars and curtained with cobwebs. Once more he had to bemoan his lost liberty. This time it was a Christian king, whom he had served, for whom he had shed his blood "on the loftiest occasion that the centuries had seen," who ordered his arrest and brought him to this bitter pass.

His imprisonment lasted from the beginning of September

to the early days of December of the year 1597. Then he regained his freedom, since his good faith and scrupulous honesty in the matter of the taxes were now established. He was released under promise to present himself in Madrid to account for a small balance of 2347 reales which remained to be justified. But he found himself so well content with the good sun of winter, lazily making its way across the gardens of Seville and the crystal of the river, that he did not proceed to Madrid within the appointed time.

Perhaps he shrank not only from a long and fruitless journey, but also from the prospect of meeting the reproachful eyes of his wife, who would call him to account, even if it were only with a look, for the loss which her little fortune might be called upon to bear through the tax-collector's bad luck, and for the days which he had spent in forgetfulness of her. Doubtless he feared Doña Catalina's displeasure more than that of judges and jailers. . . .

During the following year, he was still being pestered about his old accounts as a purveyor-delegate of Isunza's. The figures of these accounts, and those of his job as tax-collector, seem to leap from the documents and link on to one another. They form a chain of scrap-iron which twined itself round Cervantes' legs and fettered him to the end of his life.

He was now called upon to present a fresh sworn statement about his commission as tax-collector, and his dealings with all the supplies of which he had taken possession during the years 1591 and 1592. Even after this, he still could not add a full stop to the record of his troubles.

At this period, Cervantes once more had as his sole occupation that of " resident "—not now in the capital, but in the

148

more flowery city of Seville. His misadventure over his tax-collecting barred the way to any new appointment for him. The friendship and protection which his comrade Ruíz Saenz extended to him served no good purpose. It did not procure for Miguel any fresh commission on behalf of Don Gaspar de Anastro. Anastro—who had once tried to assassinate the Prince of Orange in Flanders—was Isunza's nephew, and he owed Cervantes some recompense for his self-sacrifice in that unhappy business which had cost Isunza his life.

During all this time of his commissions and his wrestling with figures and bad luck, Cervantes found scarcely any outlet through which to release the sighs of his muse. A few poor quatrains in praise of San Jacinto, which won him the first prize in an Aragonese competition, and a rhymed prose eulogy of the chief magistrate of Vizcaya, are the only known works which we owe to his genius during the whole course of the year 1595.

In the following year, Howard and Essex with an English fleet arrived off Cadiz with the object of seizing the peninsula on which the town stands. They succeeded only in carrying away some good ducats by way of ransom for leading citizens whom they took on board their ships. This event provided Cervantes with occasion to give his satiric muse an airing.

It was on 29th July that the English fleet was sighted off Cadiz. It consisted, according to the testimony of an eye-witness, of " more than forty splendid galleys, and, as all the ships had all sail set and were flying flags at bow and stern, they made a beautiful sight, which looked like a hill-side of trees afloat."

149

The writer of this description had a mind so sensitive to beauty that he forgot, as he gazed upon the spectacle, what a danger was moving upon the city in these sails before the wind, between the blue of the sky and the blue of the sea. In the gossip-centres of Sevillle, the arrival, off the neighbouring port of Cadiz, of the ships dispatched by Queen Elizabeth was commented upon with less enthusiasm for the beautiful sight of a sea sown with sails. There was more talk about the carelessness of the government, which had dismantled the port fortifications and left the city without a garrison, and about the incapacity of the commander of the Spanish fleet.

He was that same Duke of Medina Sidonia who had simply folded his arms at the time of Drake's raid in 1587, and, in his command of the "Invincible" Armada, had worried about nothing except that there should be plenty of good salt pork. Now, more interested in his lucrative tunny-fishing, he did not care that the ships under Portocarrero which were sent to meet the English were old and unseaworthy, and carried only one midship's gun apiece. It was only after the Earl of Essex had decided to evacuate the port that Medina Sidonia entered the city in triumph.

The gallantry of the people of Cadiz did not suffice to resist the English forces, who captured the city and took hostages out of whom they extracted plenty of gold; which was all they wanted, for they were not so much in quest of glory. The populace took up arms against them, since what was called the Armada was lacking in armament, and even the very friars seized spear and shield.

"All the city companies advanced out of the city, and among them a company of Franciscan friars with their pikes and banners,

150

and another company of Augustinian friars who were proceeding to the Indies, to the number of seventy."

This warlike accoutrement of monks, together with the carefree ease of the duke in the peace of his tunny-fishing, served the wits of Seville as pedestals for the curvetting of their satiric muses. Sanz de Zumeta ended a sonnet, in which he mourned the shame of the sack and ruin of Cadiz, in these ironical words:

> " When in our own despite the enemy
> Were left to sing our praises . . .
> By grace of the god of tunny ! "

And Cervantes celebrated the event in that bitter sonnet of his which is too little known, and less quoted:

> " With friars a-many war-bedight,
> July presents another Holy Week;
> But now 'tis Mars they seek.
> In company they flock, enough to fright
> The populace, if not the foe.
> Such wind they broke as blew them all,
> Within a few days, great and small,
> Away, and laid them low.
> For Mammon roared them his command,
> And earth was darkened, sea and land;
> You'd think the last trump blow.
> Then into Cadiz, feeling no whit the meaner,
> Once that the Earl did go,
> Triumphant marched the great Duke of Medina."

This sonnet of his links on to that more famous one in which he celebrated the death of Philip the Great. The occasion of the first sonnet led to the occasion of the second. The King's mortification over the rout of the " Invincible " Armada, aggravated by the sack of Cadiz, undermined his failing health, and he died a little later. From this it would appear that the Duke of Medina Sidonia—married to a daughter of the Princess of Eboli's, with whose conception, so the gossips said, the King had more to do than the prince —hastened the moment of Philip's death, since the duke's blunders shattered the hour-glass of the King's days.

The King was dead; and Miguel de Cervantes, who had received nothing at his hands but rebuffs, and who, above all, had kept worship of Don John of Lepanto alive in his heart, could not squeeze a tear out of his eyes to shed upon his virgin page in palatine poetry. He found nothing on his lips but a smile of indifference. He left it graven there; and, for Philip's epitaph, he wrote:

> " He cocked his hat, he called for his sword,
> He looked askance . . . and was gone without a word."

CHAPTER XXI

THE beginning, or the ending, of a century marked no change in Cervantes' estate, either in his outward seeming or in his inward serenity.

He was still drifting, with no lucky landfall in sight, when he left the sixteenth century behind him to enter upon the seventeenth century. He was still as unsure as ever of something to wear, somewhere to lay his head, and someone to love him. Time itself became more prodigal with its dating, since it enriched the numbering of the centuries by one. But Miguel still found himself lacking in the smallest gift to add to his scanty store.

Once again he sought the company of the luckless, since it was not given to him to enter the company of those who had inherited greatness or won it. He gossiped with bravoes and struck up acquaintance with poets whose muses were pedestrian. He contemplated the tomb erected in the cathedral of Seville to the greater glory of the late Philip II, and talked with bystanders about the dispute between the Holy Office and the High Court which had interrupted the funeral, to the detriment of the eternal repose of the King, defender of the faith by dagger and stake.

One of these days, while the people gathered round the abandoned tomb were discussing the differences between the inquisitors and the judges, " there swaggered in some poet or other who sported a stanza about the magnificence of the tomb. . . ." All very true, apart from the fact that the stanza was a sonnet, that the swaggering poet was the most humble of all poets, and that the wits of Ariño, the chronicler of this, among others, of *Sevillian Happenings*, were unequal to the task of understanding Cervantes' gentle irony.

To this period of his life belong the story of his journey in La Mancha and the fable of his imprisonment by order of the mayor Medrano at Argamasilla de Alba. It may be that Miguel was entrusted with some further tax-gathering commission or other. He was not qualified to seek his livelihood in any other occupation. Still less could he depend on the fruits of his genius, which was not yet mature, and live by his pen, whose output was still scanty. So it may be that, once again, he scoured the towns in the neighbourhood of Seville. But, if he ever went to Argamasilla, he left no trace of what he did with his time there, still less of any stay in its prison.

We do not know where, or how, this legend came to birth. Doubtless Argamasilla would like to have been the scene of his imprisonment, so that it might lay claim to being the cradle of his genius. But, unfortunately for its claims, people came along who, for love of Miguel and the truth, ransacked archives, unearthed documents, shook the dust of centuries off them, and, in so doing, scared away the timid fledgling of the La Mancha legend.

The one sure thing is that there is no more light upon this period of Cervantes' life than the light which a grating lets through a cell window. Miguel went back to prison; but the whole episode is so obscure that we cannot assign any definite reason for it or time to it. The reason, however, must have been the same old one of those accounts which were never reduced to order, those balances which were never justified; and the time must have been about the year 1602–3.

On 24th January 1604, there is a statement by my lords of the Treasury, in connection with that commission at Baza which introduced such long and wearisome colophons into the story of Cervantes' life. " In order that he might present his accounts, orders were given by Señor Bernabé de Pedroso to release him from the prison in which he was confined in Seville, under bail that he would present them within a certain period, but up to the present he has not done so. . . ."

This imprisonment of his is clearly not to be confused with the one which he suffered six years earlier; for on that occasion it was the judge Vallejo who gave orders for Miguel's release. But for this difference of names, the slow processes of justice, the similarity of the circumstances, and the identical nature of the instructions issued, might lead us to believe that my lords of the Treasury were still unaware of the fact that Cervantes had been released in 1597.

Miguel beguiled his enforced leisure in the prison of Seville by taking material from his own past at random, piecing it together with the pliant mortar of his now mature genius, and thus constructing the finest palace ever created by human imagination.

In its building his bitterness, his loneliness, his poverty sought to lend a hand. They might have made this edifice, fashioned out of such grim material, a dark mass which shut out the sun of humanity. But this sun Miguel carried within himself, and it was in vain that his sorrows strove in his imagination, for these sorrows themselves became bathed with light.

Out of that heart of his which had been wrung by life's unfairness, out of that mind of his which had known fortune's unreason, emerged a work, not of brooding rebellion, but of mild and gentle protest. It reaches our hearts in no rude hurry, with no cry of hatred, no call for revenge. It is the first, and the most sublime, fruit of that form of humour which laughs lest it should weep.

All the time that Cervantes was reflecting and writing, around him moved a strange world. Bravoes and broken men, ruffians and tricksters, passed beside him. Doubtless they supposed that, if he took any notice of them at all, he would soon forget them. How could they tell that their portraits were printed on his mind's eye, to be put down on paper and immortalised in a book?

This prison of Seville was the most populous in all Spain. The city, the gateway between one world and another, assembled the most diverse and dangerous human fauna. Some two thousand inmates were lodged within the prison walls, if one counts the lady friends of prisoners who, through the not entirely disinterested kindness of the governor and his warders, came to spend the night with their *chiquiznaques*.

This was no rigorous prison through whose gates only those who held the authority of magistrates and notaries could come and go. The governor and his turnkeys also issued free passes, which made their own purses more full and their prisoners' hours less empty. But sometimes these liberties transformed themselves into real liberty. Those who were let out might not come back. Others might make their way out with nobody's permission but their own, taking advantage of the medley of comings and goings which set the sentries' heads swimming. The mistresses of prisoners brought oranges to cheat their hunger, and stayed on in the prison to satisfy other appetites of those who hungered and thirsted, but not after righteousness.

Here—if he had not already picked them up on the *gradas*—Cervantes learnt the cant and jargon of bullies and tricksters. He discovered that the gates of the prison had the names of metals: "Gold," "silver," and "copper," because they opened and shut to the profit of turnkeys whose goodwill was for hire. He learnt that the different sections into which the prisoners were divided bore the names of "the Traitor," "the Silent File," "the Bravoes," and "the Plague."

In these haunts he heard about episodes, tragic or picaresque, which he was later to introduce into his novels. Among them was the story of the bloodthirsty Silvestre Angulo. This was afterwards to serve him as material for his denunciation, in Chapters V and VI of his *Persiles*, of those who turned jealousy into a sharp knife to end the lives of guilty wives and their lovers, and the barbarous law which authorised them to do so.

"What good do you suppose it would do you," he says through the mouth of the Pole Periander to the angry husband, "if justice handed your enemies over to you, helpless and bound, above a public square, before the eyes of a multitude of people, and you brandished a knife over the scaffold, threatening to cut their throats, as though their blood could cleanse what you call your honour? What could it do for you, except make the wrong done to you more public?"

This humane and sensible advice was inspired by an event

in the year 1565, when Silvestre Angulo, in accordance with a cruel but traditional law, put his wife and the man who had robbed him of her love and his own honour to death on a public scaffold. The prayers of the guilty parties were of no avail, nor were those of the monks who went down on their knees to him to bear witness to humility, and presented him with the Crucifix, the symbol of Pardon. Angulo brushed them all aside indignantly, and in a frightful fury plunged his sword and dagger into the defenceless bodies of his wife and her lover.

It was also while Cervantes was in prison that news arrived about the fate of the people involved in the latest attempt to bring Dom Sebastian, dead on the battlefield in Africa, to life again. Numerous were those who, since the death of the unfortunate King, had taken his name, in the hope that with its aid they might win the crown of the Portuguese kingdom.

First there was the rustic hermit of Alcazaba, a tile-maker by trade and a hermit through addiction to idleness rather than to prayer and penance. A great lady fell in love with him, and—perhaps lest she should be reproached with surrendering her charms to a peasant—gave it out that he was the king, who had escaped from the rout of his army and was now performing the seven years of penitence traditionally imposed on any Portuguese king who lost a battle. All his supporters, together with the pretender, ended on the gallows and in the galleys.

Then there was Mateo Álvarez, a native of the island of Terceira, who also turned hermit, this time rather on account of his melancholy disposition and his poor health, which impelled him to choose a dwelling far from humanity,

in the pure air of sea and mountain. He did not seek greatness, but his isolated life and the breath of rumour pointed
him out to the populace as a possible king in penitence.
Although he first denied that he was the man they supposed
and the man they wanted, in the end the demon of pride
took possession of him, and finally he yielded to the popular
desire which made him out to be Sebastian reincarnated.
This poor man, a victim to the temptation of power, died
with Christian resignation and manly courage, hardly to
be expected in one of his frail physique.

Now, lastly, there was Marco Tulio Arzón, whose purely
Roman name and whose temperament—which, being
Calabrian, was also close to the Roman—filled him with
pride and deceived him with the idea that he was called
upon to grasp a sceptre. The web of his plot implicated also
that sadly celebrated Duke of Medina Sidonia, and for this
reason alone—even if his own transgression did not augur
a bad end—Arzón might well have given himself up for
lost; for the wretched duke did not touch anything without
bringing death and disaster. The pretender was paraded
through the streets of San Lucar, and then his troubles
ended on the gallows, where he died in company with
three of his accomplices.

But the trial continued in the persons of two friars,
involved in the Calabrian's ambitions, who as priests were
not judged by the same tribunal as laymen. The Dominican
habit of one of them and the Franciscan habit of the other
served them to no purpose, except to prolong their lives,
in fear and trembling, for a few poor months. Finally Don
Luciano de Negrón, ecclesiastical judge and archdeacon of
the cathedral of Seville, condemned them to unfrocking

and to the gallows. The first sentence was carried out in Seville at the hands of the Bishop of Cadiz, Dr. Gómez Suárez de Figueroa, and the second at the hands of the public executioner, on the same spot where the Calabrian pretender and his friends had died.

This happened in October of 1603. By this time Cervantes must have been in Valladolid; but the prologue to the drama and its early scenes must have come to his ears through those who went in and out of his Sevillian prison.

There, too, by night, he must have heard the sad chanting of prisoners marching with lighted candles, in solemn procession, to show their sympathy with one of their number who was to be executed the next day. Morning and evening, from his cell, he must have listened to the less mournful voices of people cursing and swearing, in one of the drinking dens of the prison, over a shady game of cards, or wrangling over a girl or over some insulting remark or roundelay.

Everything came to the man who kept his eyes and ears open and his mouth shut: oaths and abuse, songs and laments, news, lampoons and lyrics. And all of it was later to find expression in that delightful farce of his, *The Prison of Seville*, which, for no very sound reason, has also been attributed to Cristóbal de Chaves.

When, by order of Señor Bernabé de Pedroso, Miguel de Cervantes was released from the prison of Seville, the fruit of what he overheard there had already been distilled in two tales, small in the number of their pages, but great in their perfection of form and wealth of content: *Rinconete and Cortadillo*, and *The Jealous Estremenian*.

But he also carried with him something that was not the

CERVANTES IN PRISON

reflection of what had jarred upon his senses, of what had come to him from other people's thoughts and feelings; something that mirrored his own inward light; something that had flowed in shining surges from his heart to his pen: the first part of *The Ingenuous Knight Don Quixote of La Mancha.*

In order to present those involved accounts of his once more, he had to proceed to the city where the new King, Don Philip III, had fixed his capital: Valladolid, the heart of Castile. At his temples he bore the snows of fifty-six winters; in his heart, a load of infinite bitterness, metamorphosed, by the alchemy of genius, into sublime irony; and, in his trunk, some scrawled manuscripts. His hopes foresaw only an overshadowed path. . . .

CHAPTER XXII

WHEN Miguel arrived at Valladolid, Don Francisco Gómez de Sandoval y Rojas, fifth Marquis of Denia and fourth Duke of Lerma, was master of the destinies of Spain.

Philip III was a sovereign of limited intelligence and little spirit. He liked Latin prayers better than epic poems. He preferred the mournful sermons of Dominican and Jesuit Fathers to reports on the affairs of Flanders and on the details of administration in his own State. He spent more time on his knees, before the image of the bleeding Christ, than seated on his throne, giving audience to ministers and ambassadors, as his duty required.

Archbishop Loaysa, charged with developing his mind, and the Marquis of Velada, charged with developing his body by martial exercises, had found less fruitful soil in him than the pious Friar Antonio de Cáceres, charged with watching over his conscience. In the eyes of Loaysa and Velada, Philip was a bad pupil; in the eyes of Father Antonio, he was a model of devotion.

In Philip's own eyes, perhaps one of the greatest merits of the Duke of Lerma—apart from the fact that he had liberally relieved the penury from which the prince suffered during the lifetime of the king his father—was that Lerma was the grandson of that holy man, paragon alike of knights and monks, who was called in the world Don Francisco de Borja, Duke of Gandía and Marquis of Lombay, and later, on the altars, was to be left with only the first part of his name, together with the glorious prefix " Saint."

162

But the people were untouched by the mystical flame that burned in the King's heart. Nuns' gallants, like our Portuguese gentleman Pinheiro da Veiga, frequented churches and convent locutories with more desire to see a pretty face than a bleeding image, and more desire to listen to sweet words than to a penitential sermon. Even those who had no nun to whom to pay court, as the tolerance of Superiors and custom permitted, went to church functions rather for gossip than for prayer. Pinheiro himself, in his description of a famous ceremony in the church of Santa Maria Magdalena, on that saint's day, interposes this passage:

" At this moment, along came a very pretty girl. There was no room for her, for the church was very crowded, and the friar said to the old woman: ' Señora, would you make room for this maiden, who is a penitent of mine? '

" The old woman replied: ' If she has a Father like you for her confessor, she must be as maiden as her mother.'

" Whereupon the girl asked: ' And what do you see about me to make you say that? '

" The old woman answered: ' I see, my dear young lady, that you have a very pretty face and a very shapely body.'

" To which one of those present replied: ' There are plenty of other pretty women in the church. Do you suggest that none of them is good? '

" The old woman answered: ' Nobody but the glorious Magdalene and myself—both of us made out of dry old wood.'

" Then the fat priest got up and invited the girl to sit on the leather bench, since they would not make room for her elsewhere.

" She replied: ' Excuse me, but it is very hot, and I do not want to put myself between skin and flesh, as somebody else said.' Because, when two priests in a carriage in the Prado, one of them much given to Bacchus and the other to Venus, invited a masked girl to come for a drive with them, she replied : ' That would be putting myself between the skin and the flesh.'

" In the end, she and her mother agreed to sit down on the bench

163

among us, saying that they would rather be ' with ordinary people, instead of with the devil and the flesh, like those others (the priests).' The service was one long laugh, thanks to the friar ; so much so that they sent from the choir to ask us to keep quiet; but Father Tiedra did not suffice to silence him, and we delighted to listen to him and would not let go of him."

It was not only church services, but also morals, which required greater discipline, as this passage clearly shows. But, despite the severe authority of the ascetic king, Valladolid went its own way, with all its freedom of speech, customs and behaviour. In the book of the Portuguese writer, entitled *Fastiginia*, which we might call a mirror of effrontery and loose living, some scarcely edifying incidents are related, such as the sale of a girl which was registered " in Valladolid on the 25th of March of this present year 1604."

In this sale contract—which must have reminded Miguel very closely of the deed which gifted his sister Andrea to Giovanni Francisco Leocadelo—it was set forth that

" in view of the many obligations which he owes, and expects to owe henceforth, to the Señora Doña Ana de Valles, unmarried daughter of the said Señora Doña Francisca, and in fulfilment of a certain promise and contract between them, to which the witnesses hereunder subscribing and signing bear testimony, he conveys and agrees that he owes to the said señora one thousand ducats, reckoned at eleven reales to the ducat, which he contracts to give and assign to her in jewellery and good money. . . ."

In the parks of the Espolón and the Prado, gallants and veiled ladies conversed with as little reticence on their lips as in their eyes. In many a house, girls, indifferently chaperoned by servants who deliberately turned a blind eye, entertained the beaux who came to court them on pretext of inquiring for their health and bringing dainties for their palates, though it was other appetites that they satisfied as well.

By no means all lips sang the praises of the Duke of Lerma and the royal favour which he enjoyed. The Augustinian monk Castroverde made such slighting remarks about the duke's control of the King's ear that he earned himself four years' banishment from the capital. But most people, indeed the great majority, if they had had to put their thoughts into words, would have congratulated the King upon making such a deserving choice, and fawned upon the duke—even though their unspoken thoughts might be of a very different colour.

It was in this state of laxity of morals, and also in a state of administrative confusion, that Cervantes found Valladolid, capital of the Spains by grace, and thanks to the whim, of the royal favourite, whose own estates were close to it. Valladolid was now the capital; and, as such, it swarmed with men in jobs, and men out of jobs.

Miguel had gone there because he was summoned to render, once again, those accounts of his which never came to a full stop, never reached their final settlement. But he went there, too, no doubt, in the hope that he would be luckier with King Philip III than he had been with his late father; for hope, even if it be but a weak, wan reflection of itself, always gleams in men's minds until the light fades from their minds too.

On his way to Valladolid, Miguel stopped at Esquivias, and at the former capital, Madrid. In the one place, he saw his wife; in the other, his sister Magdalena and his illegitimate daughter, Isabel de Saavedra.

By this time the years, like rain falling upon crude statuary, had smoothed away the rougher edges of their hearts. Catalina's heart no longer preserved the asperity of her younger days. Her middle-aged, maimed husband was her last refuge, her sole remaining source of affection, upon earth. They could speak the language of love together now: a love purified, by time and trouble, of all passion, all bitterness. For the first time in his life, perhaps, Miguel de Cervantes, now nearing his sixties, found the way to his wife's heart.

So full of forgiveness was it, so ready for any sacrifice, that she agreed to accept the company of the girl whose birth reminded her that lips other than her own had kissed Miguel's now shrivelled lips: his illegitimate daughter. Doña Catalina, Magdalena and Isabel arranged to accompany Cervantes, the head of the family, to the capital, where his other sister Andrea was now living. She had been left a widow, and had taken up dressmaking for a livelihood.

In Madrid Cervantes also went to see Francisco de Robles, the bookseller. With Robles he came to terms about the publication of that other work which he had in his baggage, and which was entitled *The Ingenuous Knight Don Quixote of La Mancha*. He had still to give it a final polishing, so that it might present itself to the world perfected in plot and phrasing.

The bookseller doubtless read some chapters of it and found it amusing, with its narrative of comical misadventures and its racy dialogue well worked in together. But he is not likely to have perceived the light that shone in the background of it; for probably the author himself had not realised that, as he wrote it, the star-dust of his imagination

166

kept falling on his paper. It was a work of genius, in short, and, as in all such cases, the author did not know it for what it was. He intended only to divert his readers with a mild satire on the craze for books about knight-errantry.

Miguel de Cervantes presumably lived in Valladolid throughout the year 1603; but there is no record or proof of his stay there at this time except one or two bills for sewing and ironing, presented by his sister Andrea and put into writing by the same hand which wrote *Don Quixote*. Even these documents do not bear faithful witness, for they lack what would carry the greatest conviction to our minds: the name of the city where they were drawn up. It may just as well have been the former capital, Madrid.

During the early months of his stay in Valladolid, Miguel devoted himself painstakingly to polishing the original of his manuscript. He talked about it to the bookseller Robles, who kept open house in Valladolid, and was sometimes to be found there and sometimes in Madrid. He mentioned the approaching publication of his *Ingenuous Knight* at literary gatherings. So the fame of his still unborn hero passed from mouth to mouth until it was known all over the city and even elsewhere in Spain.

There was talk about *Don Quixote* even before the printer Cuesta had put it upon his machines; but not all tongues praised the work of its author. His youth had produced no very striking fruits, and this fact alone sufficed to cast doubts upon the quality of his maturer inspiration.

With these pleasant pursuits Cervantes alternated work which bored him, but which he had to do for the sake of the money it brought him. He executed commissions for

167

friends of his who were away from the capital, but had interests there: Don Fernando de Toledo; the Portuguese Simón Méndez, later to become of unhappy memory in his life; Bartolomé de Pedroso, then treasury councillor, and others.

He also wasted many an hour in the favourite's ante-rooms, to see whether at last he could obtain some recompense for his services to the late king; but neither flattery—if he tried any—nor argument—if he found any opportunity for it—served him any better with Philip III than with Philip II.

In July 1604 Miguel's mother-in-law died, and he had to go to Esquivias, where his presence, and his signature, were required for the division of her inheritance. It was divided with a sharp priestly eye to the main chance, in order to make sure that, if Doña Catalina died, her property should not go to Cervantes, but to his brother-in-law, the cleric Don Francisco Palacios.

In August Miguel and his wife went to Toledo, where they had to sell some land which she had inherited. In Toledo, at this time, resided Lope de Vega, recently married to Doña Juana de Guardo.

Already, at the time of his stay in Seville, Cervantes had had occasion to observe that neither himself nor his work was *persona grata* in the eyes of Lope de Vega, that phœnix of literature. There was no reasonable ground for this enmity between the two of them. But perhaps it went against the grain for Miguel to see a man deified, during his lifetime, whose merits he knew to be lower than his own, at least in depth of thought and capacity for writing fine prose; whereas nobody sang Miguel's praises and fawned upon him, nor had the fruits of his imagination earned him wealth, or even a home.

Perhaps Lope de Vega, on his side, thought that Miguel had too much to say about his love affairs. Perhaps he was jealous lest his popularity should be threatened by the appearance on the horizon of a reputation greater than his own, and better founded. In any case, he tried to bar Miguel's path to fame with sarcasm and innuendo.

There are always go-betweens in the jealousies and rivalries of great men, who, with the best of good intentions, carry their scornful or spiteful sayings from the one to the other. Even before the printing-press had made the fact common property, Lope de Vega was already aware that a chapter in the *Ingenuous Knight* embodied Miguel de Cervantes' poor opinion of his work. He was also acquainted with some other references to himself in the prologue and the verses with which Miguel adorned the opening pages of his immortal book.

"In one line they depict a distracted lover," Cervantes writes, with Lope de Vega's *Pilgrim in his Fatherland* evidently in his mind, " and in the next line they proclaim a Christian sentiment which it is a delight to hear or read." After this passage comes one in which Cervantes speaks of the humility of his own book, and declares that it is not " one of those that are full of quotations from Aristotle, Plato and the whole galaxy of philosophers, which readers admire so much and which make them take the authors for learned, erudite and eloquent men."

Cervantes jeers wittily at the childish parade of erudition on the part of some vacuous authors, and proceeds to make fun of the faults of construction in Lope de Vega's novels.

Even the praises of his own book with which Cervantes fills the beginning of it—praises signed with outlandish names, though he confesses that they are all from his own pen—are nothing but a satire on the dithyrambs which Lope de Vega prints at the beginning of his books and which, though he attributes them to various writers, are simply shameless inventions of his own.

All the embers of their old enmity were fanned into flame by this combustible material. Lope repaid Miguel in his own coin of sarcasm and contempt. But Lope was daring enough to condemn a book which, so far, he only knew from extracts, since it was not yet published. On 14th August of this year 1604, he wrote a letter to a friend of his, in which he wrapped up a stone to be hurled against the pedestal of Cervantes' reputation:

> "About authors I say nothing. This is a good season for them. Many are blossoming out in the coming year, but none so bad as Cervantes, or so foolish as to praise his *Don Quixote*."

Now Cervantes and Lope de Vega were both at Toledo. These two men, who might have understood one another and given one another mutual support against other people's misunderstanding and hostility, probably did not meet; but they knew what they thought about one another, thanks to the tittle-tattle of busybodies and sycophants. So here, in open hatred, ended a relationship which, at the beginning, promised to be a sincere friendship, in those days when, in his *Galatea*, Cervantes praised the work of de Vega in his song to Calliope. Since then, they had drifted further and further apart, with jealousy to keep each of them company, until they had come to this pass.

When Cervantes went back to Valladolid, he thought

about whom he should choose as patron for his book: the patron who should

"graciously take it under his protection, so that, under his shelter, although it lacks that precious adornment of elegance and erudition usually worn by works composed in the houses of men who know everything, it may dare to make its appearance, despite the judgment of some people who, *undeterred by the limitations of their own ignorance, are in the habit of condemning other people's works with much severity, but less fairness*."

In other words, as Cervantes broadly hints, he hoped that respect for the name of his patron would give pause to the evil-speaking tongues of Lope's chorus.

Cervantes' choice for his patron fell upon Señor Don Alonso Diego López de Zúñiga y Sotomayor, Duke of Béjar, a man of about thirty, and a rich one at least in ducats, if not in brains. His wife, the very noble Señora Doña Juana Mendoza, daughter of the Duke del Infantado, helped him to spend the money which had been left to him by other men, cleverer at amassing it, but not so skilled in getting rid of it.

Of his poverty of intellect we have clear proof in this anecdote, which passed from mouth to mouth, and was then set down by Don Juan de Arguijo in his amusing collection of anecdotes: "About the Duke of Béjar, who died in the year 1620," Arguijo writes, "somebody remarked that he had died like a saint. Somebody else replied: 'Doubtless he has gone straight to Heaven, unless nothingness has claimed him for its own.'"

This Duke of Béjar—whose name would never have got into print but for this anecdote, which consecrates him as a nitwit, and for Cervantes' dedication of his book to him

—did not show any gratitude to the man who rescued him from oblivion and handed him down the centuries. There is no record that he ever extended his patronage either to the book or to its author: to the one, by taking it under the protection of his social prestige; to the other, by bestowing largess upon Cervantes.

In this hope, as in so many others in the course of his life, Cervantes was disappointed. Never again did he mention the Duke of Béjar in the prologues and dedications of his books. He dedicated them thereafter only at the moment of going to press, and so much as a mere matter of form that, in his dedication of one of them to the Marquis of Ayamonte, he even borrows Fernando de Herrera's phraseology.

There may have been a reason for the disdain with which the duke received Cervantes' offering. Ill will against Miguel did not have to kick its heels in the ante-rooms of the great. It was given easy access to them from the government offices and the chophouses where those who spoke badly of him were alike to be found. Doubtless somebody was not lacking who refreshed the duke's memory and reminded him of the sonnet composed by the author of *Don Quixote*, in which he referred with witty daring to the "conquest" of Cadiz by the Duke of Medina Sidonia, who happened to be an uncle of the Duke of Béjar's.

The Duke of Béjar may have cherished resentment over the disrespectful way in which a poetaster had dared to speak about such an important personage, who was related to him not only by blood but also by their common lack of brains. But we may also suppose that somebody else was not very far away from the ducal household at this time, and that the slamming of the door of the ducal heart against largess for genius in distress was not unconnected with the intrigues of that other genius, that imp of mischief, Lope de Vega, who was a welcome guest at the Béjares, as he was at the Lemos and the Saldañas.

A more fruitful friendship—although it was to yield its fruit only in the winter of his life—was the one which Cervantes renewed at this time with the Lord Archbishop of Toledo, Cardinal Don Bernando de Sandoval y Rojas. Their friendship had been born years before from a song of pompous eulogy which Miguel wrote about him. At the end of his life, when Cervantes found himself poor and forgotten, it was to be the Cardinal who helped him most in his troubles.

Meanwhile, if he obtained anything from the prelate it was only fair words and good counsel. We know of no employment which helped him along through these needy days of his in the new capital. Nor is there any foundation for the belief that he was entrusted with writing the official narrative of the celebrations which took place in connection with the arrival of an English embassy, with the object of negotiating an alliance, and the coincident birth of the royal prince who was later to become the poet-king, Philip IV of Spain.

The Englishman who arrived in Valladolid as ambassador extraordinary was the same man who had dispersed what was left of the Armada, the same man who had seized Cadiz, carried off hostages, and held them to ransom: Lord Howard of Effingham, Lord High Admiral of England. But these were not days for remembering grudges, but for forgetting them.

173

Hopes ran high that, in addition to the brocades, laces, velvets, gold and precious stones with which the English—and the Spanish—gentlemen adorned themselves, the embassy would be further adorned by a marriage which would unite the reigning Houses of Habsburg and Stuart. Hopes ran high, too, that the prince who had just been born to Philip III and his queen would prove the redeemer awaited by Spain, who would once more school the sun to paint the name of Iberia with its golden rays upon all the horizons of the world.

But the expected marriage did not take place; nor did the Spanish Messiah arrive.

It all ended in tourneys and balls, which were described with the utmost elegance by the learned Portuguese writer Pinheiro da Veiga in his famous *Fastiginia*, and with no less elegance and also sarcasm, although with more conciseness, by Luis de Góngora, in his sonnet:

" Our Queen gave birth; then came the Lutheran,
　　With heretics by the hundred in his train.
　　We flung our money gaily down the drain
　　To feed and fête the man.

　　And jousts like mad we joined in;
　　And gorged, not over-wise,
　　To honour her and all her spies—
　　That Queen by grace of Calvin.

　　The boy, we said, a gift of God was,
　　Or so we hoped for Spain.
　　Now Luther's rich and we, alas,
　　Are left lamenting our poor pass.
　　All this they wrote with might and main,
　　Don Quixote, Sancho and his ass."

The end of this sonnet has misled some people into the belief that a commission to describe the celebrations came to Cervantes, arm in arm with Don Quixote, by way of relieving the penury in his home for a few months. But anybody who assumes this misses the satirical intention of the poet. He is simply branding as madmen and asses the people who spent so much money in honour of the born enemies of their faith and country. It is easy to see, moreover, that anybody who makes such an assumption has not read the actual *Narrative of events in the city of Valladolid.* It is a compilation without grace or style, rambling and boring, which could never have been even a distant relation of the *Ingenuous Knight.*

That work saw the light during the early days of the year of grace 1605.

CHAPTER XXIII

IT is through the medium of a *cause célèbre*, which embittered the sweets of the success that his book achieved in its first edition, that we know exactly where Miguel was living, and even who his neighbours were, in these early days of the year 1605.

In addition to his sister Andrea and his niece Doña Constanza de Ovando, who had been living with him since his arrival in the capital, he now had with him also his wife Doña Catalina, his sister Magdalena, and his illegitimate daughter Isabel de Saavedra, who had first come into his home as a servant, but later took her proper place as daughter in it. They lived in an apartment in a house belonging to Juan de las Navas, in the Rastro, near the little gate of the Esgueva.

The house, a recently built one, was what was known as a tenement house. On the first floor lived Doña Luisa de Montoya, widow of the royal annalist Esteban de Garibay. Opposite her lived the Cervantes family.

On the ground floor there was a chophouse or tavern, and on the floor above them lived Doña Juana Gaitan, widow of the poet Lainez, with some young and pretty relations and god-children of hers. In another apartment on the same floor lived Doña Mariana Ramírez, who was on good terms—which some people made so bold as to say passed the limits of friendship—with Don Diego de Miranda. In the attics lived one Doña Isabel de Ayala, a busybody with a glib tongue.

176

CERVANTES' HOUSE IN EL TOBOSO

In this house, in which the only men were the two Garibay sons and the veteran of Lepanto, the first months of the year 1605 passed amid gossiping and backbiting, dubious friendships, furtive visits, whispering behind doors and squinting through cracks in them. It must have been a regular house of ill fame, if it matched the temperaments of most of its inhabitants and the very free and easy morals of the great city which had become the capital of the Spains.

Probably the only respectable, the only unmasked visitors who entered its doors were the Genoese contractor Agustín Ragio and Simón Méndez, Portuguese by birth and now treasurer-general of shipping dues, who came to chat with Cervantes about old times in Seville or help him to reckon up his advances on royalties.

Be this as it may, Miguel, up in the clouds of his first triumph, which in a few days had set him and his work on the road to fame, paid no attention to his neighbours. Stories of intrigues and love affairs had nothing to do with him. His own apartment had to be quiet and well run, not only in order to conform with the loftiness of his thoughts and the exalted rank which his name already held among the famous, but also, and above all, in order to conform with the Christian character of his wife, Doña Catalina de Palacios, and her close calculation of housekeeping expenses.

By this time the dream of some wealthy marriage for sister Magdalena had gone the way of all dreams; and, if the two marriageable girls of the family, the cousins Constanza and Isabel, talked about boys and betrothals, it was in the purest and most childlike way, under the close guardianship of the three ladies who were their elders and their betters in knowledge of the world.

It must have been a very quiet, chaste life, this life of a family gathered together under the protection of a broken man, in the midst of other families whose example—apart from that of their religious neighbours the Garibays—could scarcely be taken as a model for decent living.

Morning prayer, with Mass on the appointed days; needlework during the day-time, to eke out the family resources; some good reading aloud at night, by the flickering light of a lamp, whose guttering wick made an unpleasant accompaniment to the spoken word; memories of other days, recalled without regret now that they were gone; and, when silence spread its gentle waves over tired minds, the rustle of finished dressmaking jobs—and the scraping of a pen, writing away in the next room.

The escudos which Miguel received from the bookseller Robles, derived from the first sale of his book and from concessions for its sale in the various kingdoms of Spain, sufficed to make this quiet life in the veteran's home more pleasant. His circumstances were still straitened, but he was no longer in actual poverty.

Within a few months *Don Quixote* attained an unexpectedly large sale. A copy of the celebrated book was to be seen in everybody's hands. Everybody felt the better of the hearty, healthy laughter to which he was moved by the tale of the comical misadventures of the Ingenuous Knight.

On 12th April in Valladolid, Cervantes signed a codicil to his contract with Francisco de Robles which empowered the bookseller to sell his book in the kingdoms of Portugal, Aragon, Valencia and Catalonia. The dispatch of copies to the New World followed shortly afterwards. This fact shows very clearly how rapidly the reputation of the book had spread, for we must bear in mind how few were the readers who could be counted upon at that time in the young cities overseas.

Within a few months of the publication of the book, there was scarcely anybody who had not heard of those creatures of Cervantes' imagination, Don Quixote and Sancho Panza. People talked about what they had to say, repeated their witty remarks, and even went so far as to give them embodiment in masquerades and festivals, or apply their names to acquaintances who presented features similar to those which Cervantes attributed to his characters.

Lest anything should be lacking in his glory, it inflicted wounds of jealousy; and, out of these wounds, those who suffered from them extracted gall, which they discharged in anonymous letters.

" While I was in Valladolid," writes Cervantes himself, " they brought a letter to my house, with a real to pay on it for postage. A niece of mine accepted it and paid the fee. She will never get it back. But, in justification of this, I may say that many a time she had heard me say that there are three ways in which only too much money is wasted : in giving alms, in paying doctors, and in accepting letters not prepaid. Let my friends take warning from this, and let my enemies know what I purpose to do.

" They gave me the letter, and inside it I found a bad sonnet, a feeble one, with no elegance or wit about it, criticising *Don Quixote*. But what troubled me was the payment of a real for this ; and I made up my mind henceforth never to accept letters on which there was a charge to pay."

But this pale radiance of a life doomed to darkness soon waned, for fresh troubles and trials were lying in ambush for Cervantes round Time's corner.

A Navarrese gentleman, by name Don Gaspar de Espeleta, had come to Valladolid for the royal festivities. More of a philanderer than a master of horsemanship and arms, he enjoyed better luck with lovelorn ladies than with gentlemen noted in the bull-ring and the lists, and he showed to better advantage in witty conversation than in fighting bulls or unhorsing knights. About him and his poor showing in a tourney Góngora had written, in derisory strain :

> " Let us sing—what theme greater ?—
> Let us not weep at all
> For the shameful fall
> Of Don Gaspar de Espeleta.
> Oh, if I could but write a lay
> Worthy of the role
> Of a thing so droll,
> At least I would say
> That the intruder fell,
> By the look of the wight,
> Because he was no knight.
> I should say as well
> That, little in the lists,
> Often the ground he's kissed.
> If in January he fell,
> He'd be honoured with Paul ;
> Though 'tis true, after all,
> When God saved him from Hell,
> Paul fell in a blaze,
> While he fell in a maze."

But his lack of address as a horseman did not deprive him of the affection of the ladies, who were not attracted by courage and skill in the lists of arms, but by the grace of God made manifest in looks and carriage. That other requisite for success in the lists of love, fine clothes, was assured to Don Gaspar, poor gentleman though he was, by the friendship and favour of Don Diego de Croy y Penlín, Marquis of Falces, who entertained him at table and lent him his own finery.

With this gentleman the wife of a notary, named Galbán, fell in love. Her husband came to hear about his wife's straying, and tried to put an end to it by peaceful means before resorting to strong measures. Relatives mediated, priests intervened, and the notary's wife promised to forget the gentleman of Navarre. But her intention to stick to the path of duty did not get beyond words and promises. Very soon it became known that Espeleta's relations with Galbán's wife had been renewed, doubtless more ardently than ever after their enforced separation.

This information brought the adventures of the gentleman of Navarre to a full stop, and started a new series of tribulations for Miguel de Cervantes Saavedra.

The husband and relatives of Espeleta's lady friend threatened the persistent gallant with death. He was aware of his danger, and took measures to protect himself.

During the evening of 27th June of this year 1605, Don Gaspar de Espeleta left the house where he was lodging, which was that of the widow Juana Ruiz in the Calle de los Monteros, and proceeded, accompanied by two of his pages, to the palace of the Marquis of Falces. He arrived there about six o'clock, and had to wait for the Marquis, who was out. When the Marquis returned, they went for a ride together, as was their custom, and spent an hour or two together until after nightfall.

About ten o'clock, after leaving the Marquis's home, Don Gaspar sent one of his pages to fetch his sword and shield. Then he exchanged his long cape for the page's short cloak, and, thus disguised, proceeded to his amorous rendezvous for that night. The place must have been somewhere near the house where Cervantes lived. This fact was known to the man who was lying in wait to kill Don Gaspar.

This assassin—so a servant at the house next door to Miguel's afterwards stated—was a man with a round face and a short, well-trimmed red beard. He was short, and wore black breeches and a tunic open at the neck, which revealed his white shirt and vandyke collar of the same colour.

Cervantes had already gone to bed when he heard somebody rousing his neighbour, the priest Luis de Garibay, and telling him that there was a man in the street calling for help. Miguel went down to the street in company with the two Garibay brothers. They found Don Gaspar de Espeleta lying bathed in blood and loudly calling for a confessor.

The two brothers picked the wounded man up and carried him to their room, where they made him as comfortable as they could on a mattress laid in the middle of it. Then they informed the officers of the law and his relative or friend, whichever he might be, the Marquis of Falces.

In the name of the law arrived the city magistrate, Don Cristóbal Villarroel, who was later to show himself so biased and so poor a friend of the justice which he represented. The Marquis brought his friend consolation and also a surgeon to do what he could for him.

But Don Gaspar de Espeleta had received two mortal wounds, one in the thigh and the other in the stomach. He may have needed consolation, which is always a good

182

thing, even for those who have nothing else to hope for in this world; but he had no use for the surgeon and his arts, which were powerless to stay his soul, already taking leave of him in groans and gushes of blood.

Don Gaspar died two days later in the home of Garibay's widow, Doña Luisa Montoya, tended by that good woman, by Andrea, Cervantes' sister, and by the surgeon Sebastián Macías, formerly surgeon to His Majesty's horse guards. The dying man did not say from whom he had received his wounds. He declared that his attacker was unknown to him, and that the two of them had fought fairly and honourably, as befitted gentlemen.

In Don Gaspar's pocket the magistrate Villarroel found a letter. Having read it, he put it into his own pocket. He made no further use of it, nor was it mentioned in the course of the proceedings.

Doubtless it gave him a clue to the truth; but the light of the truth was so blinding that he shut his eyes to it and looked elsewhere. This bad judge did not choose to be brought face to face with the truth, lest he should also be brought face to face with Galbán the notary, who belonged to his own legal caste and had influence at the palace—in other words, influence over promotion or dismissal.

Accordingly Villarroel must have blessed that worthy gentleman Espeleta, who died without revealing the name of his assailant. Accordingly he must have cursed one of the dead man's pages, Francisco Camporredondo, and wished him dead too a thousand times over. For this page was of no mind to keep his mouth shut about what he had tucked away in his mind. He declared that his master had a love affair with a married woman; that he had often accompanied his master to her house, where Don Gaspar had remained; and that she was the wife of Galbán the notary, who on this account had once threatened Espeleta with death, and so had his relatives.

This declaration was confirmed by a statement by one of Don Gaspar's lackey's, who said that his master was in the habit of going to a house near the Santisteban gate, though he did not know to whom the house belonged or why Don Gaspar went there.

But that magistrate of infamous memory, Don Cristóbal Villarroel, in order to justify his existence, had to direct his activity against somebody. He did not find it convenient to turn it into the channels so clearly pointed out to him by Espeleta's servitors. Instead, he spread his net on the spot where he had found the bleeding body of the murdered man, and involved in it those who were sleeping quietly when the sword claimed its victim, and left their beds to go to his aid when they heard him calling for help.

Because he was deliberately keeping them shut, the magistrate's eyes were not opened either by the declaration made by Juana Ruiz, with whom Espeleta had lodged. She was now dying herself, and, to ease her conscience, she desired to tell the magistrate all that she knew of the truth.

In response to the dying woman's request, two constables, accompanied by a scrivener, went to her bedside. She informed them that Don Gaspar had long had a love-affair with a married woman, and told them his mistress' name and her husband's profession. Their relations had suffered eclipse for some little time through a conjugal storm, in which the lightning of the husband's anger flashed and threatened to strike. But the storm blew over, and they renewed their guilty intercourse. In Don Gaspar's pocket were to be found two rings which the lady had given him. He had returned them to her during their brief rupture. When their relations were resumed, the gallant had got them back and kept them, despite the fact that, when the notary noticed that they were gone again, "he had threatened to kill his wife and had beaten her."

Even this statement of the dying woman's might have been dismissed by the magistrate, were it not for the fact that it found weighty support in the presence of two veiled women in Juana Ruiz's house when the two constables and the scrivener sent by his worship entered it. One of them was on her knees and weeping.

Who these women were nobody knew except the magistrate himself. They were summoned into his presence and there unveiled. They may well have been Galbán's wife and a servant of hers. Galbán's wife may have heard that Juana Ruiz was going to make a statement, and gone to her house to ask her not to compromise her by revealing her name.

Juana Ruiz revealed it, but the skilled hand of the magistrate brushed it aside like an importunate fly. These two veiled women who were brought before him, one of them most probably the woman to whom the finger of all the evidence pointed, went back home; and no explanation of why and how they were at the dying woman's bedside ever figured in the proceedings.

What mysterious hand was it that bandaged the eyes of the magistrate Villarroel, stopped his ears, and dulled his wits? Not only did he pay no attention to statements

which would have led him to the truth; he did not even
busy himself about hunting down the actual assassin.

It is true that he gave general orders that inquiries should
be made in hospitals and monasteries where the mysterious
short man with the round face and the unbuttoned tunic
might have sought refuge if he were wounded. But the
magistrate overlooked the fact that there was a tavern on
the ground floor of the very house to which the assassin's
victim was taken, and that there was a chophouse not far
away which might equally have given the assassin shelter.
No search was made in these possible lairs, which were in
the habit of taking in bullies and sharpers, and the assassin
escaped, not so much into the darkness of the night as into
the darkness in the magistrate's conscience.

But in the case of any crime, so the magistrate said to
himself, there is always somebody to arrest. In the attics of
the Cervantes' house lived that evil-tongued Doña Isabel de
Ayala, who spied from her watchtower upon all comings
and goings, and clad even the whitest of innocent doings in
the black cloak of her foul mind. She came and poured her
venom into the proceedings, and so provided the bad judge
with somebody against whom he could discharge his
adroitly drafted " whereases."

In the eyes of this harpy, nobody was clean. It was a
question not only of her neighbours on the second floor,
women all by themselves who were frequently visited by
well-dressed gentlemen, but also of her neighbours on
the first floor, who lived such quiet, respectable lives. The
widow Garibay, with one son a priest and the other only a
boy of fifteen; and the family of Miguel de Cervantes,
which combined exemplary behaviour with its head's pre-

eminence in the republic of letters, alike found their honour at the mercy of the old witch's sharp claws.

Once he had heard the Ayala woman's evidence, the magistrate had nothing left to do but imprison the lot of them, if not for suspected complicity in Espeleta's murder, at least by way of punishment for loose living.

So Cervantes went back to prison once more. But now it was with the added grief of knowing that those devout women, in whose affection and care he had found repose after his weary life's journey, were his companions in misfortune, hanging their heads lest anyone should see the stigma set on their brows by the accusation of a vile tongue.

CHAPTER XXIV

THE gravest charge against the Cervantes family, apart from their suspected complicity in Don Gaspar de Espeleta's murder, was based on the frequent visits which Simón Méndez paid to them. Doña Isabel de Ayala pointed to him as the lover of the other Isabel, Cervantes' daughter.

"In another apartment," she says in her evidence, "live Miguel de Cervantes, and Doña Andrea and Doña Magdalena his sisters, and a daughter of the said Miguel de Cervantes, illegitimate, named Doña Isabel; and in it also lives Doña Constanza, daughter of the said Doña Andrea; and in this apartment, where the said Miguel de Cervantes and his daughter, sisters and niece live, meetings take place and gentlemen are received, whom this witness does not know, apart from the fact that their presence is a cause for scandal and talk; and among them one Simón Méndez, a Portuguese, who, to common knowledge and notoriety, lives in a state of concubinage with the said Doña Isabel, daughter of the said Miguel de Cervantes; and this witness has frequently reproached the said Simón Méndez with the fact, though he says that he visits there only because he is a friend of the family; and this witness knows, from having heard it said publicly, that the said Simón Méndez gave her a skirt which cost him more than two hundred ducats."

This sanctimonious Isabel, who lived a life of retirement in her attic, doubtless because her neighbours showed her the cold shoulder, was determined to avenge herself upon them for her enforced solitude, by forcing herself upon them now and spitting the venom of her tongue in their faces.

All the families who lived in the house were smirched by her spite, without distinction between those whom public opinion regarded as respectable and those who were not so regarded. By a miracle of ill-will, she managed to distort the humane action of the Cervantes and the Garibays and turn it against them. She did more : even the other families, which had had nothing whatever to do with the crime, even out of kindness, found their hands stained with blood and their brows branded with the mark of infamy, just because the old witch's vile tongue so depicted them.

The magistrate was nevertheless afraid lest even she, carried away by the truth, might point towards the guilty parties. He wanted to turn her evidence against some innocent party, and he asked her whether the quarrel might have arisen over some love affair in the house. She replied that

> " this witness can only affirm that she has heard it said that this was the reason of it; but she cannot say whom the quarrel was about, nor has she heard who was the man with whom the said Don Gaspar fought, nor has she any suspicion; for this witness has never had anything to do with the women in the house, because, as she has already said, their addiction to gossiping and their loose living always seemed to her a bad thing and a cause for scandal."

She did not dare to make any definite accusation, because she was afraid of suffering the pangs of a guilty conscience and the flames of Hell. But she sprang the trap of her suspicions, just like a naughty boy who sticks flints in a rosette and then assumes an air of innocence to avert detection and punishment.

This was all the magistrate wanted. Doña Isabel's ill-concealed desire to injure people whom she hated, for no other reason than that the milk of human kindness had gone sour in her, fitted in well enough with his own desire to clear the real culprit, either because he was under personal obligations to Galbán or because he had been given an official hint to do so.

So the Cervantes found themselves in prison, without even the bitter consolation of knowing that they were there just because a magistrate had so far forgotten his duty as to shut his eyes deliberately, whereas Justice herself tears the bandage from her eyes, so that she may see clearly and look around her for the guilty party. Miguel was not aware whether he was accused of complicity in Espeleta's murder or sheltering the assassin, or suspected of being the murderer himself. He could scarcely imagine that he and his family were being kept in prison on a charge of loose living.

When they were brought before the magistrate, all the women who sheltered under the author's patched cloak swore that there was no regular male visitor to their home except Símon Méndez, and that he came there " about certain sureties which they had asked him to take in the kingdom of Toledo for rents receivable from there, and that he came *for no other reason*." The most injured party of all, young Isabel herself, was asked by the magistrate, with a great deal of hemming and hawing, whether she was on terms of particular friendship and intimacy with Simón Méndez. She replied that " she denied it, because never had Simón Méndez come to her said father's house for any such purpose, nor had it ever been suggested or implied; and that she swore."

Espeleta's will contained a grateful gift to " Magdalena Cervantes." The magistrate chose to regard this posthumous present and the words which accompanied it—" because of my great affection for her "—as proof of further concubinage in the Cervantes family, and a further stain on the family whom he was trying.

It was true that a Magdalena Cervantes had tended Espeleta during his last hours. But the magistrate did not stop to reflect that she wore the dress of a devotee, and that the bequest of a silk gown was clearly not intended for her, but for some other woman who had the same name. He was bent on treating all the women of the family as procuresses and prostitutes.

The whole trial was smeared with the venemous spittle of an old busybody and stained by the dark designs of an arbitrary magistrate. When the time came for sentence to be pronounced, the three higher judges, Melchior de Teves, Alonso de Otalora and Pedro Muñoz, may not have paid overmuch attention to the documents in the case, for they were busy men; but they were not in so much of a hurry that they failed to see that prejudice had entered into the proceedings. Nor were they so blind as Villarroel would have liked them to be.

But, on the principle " you scratch my back, and I'll scratch yours," they did not care to disclose the illegality and injustice of their colleague. They proceeded to overstep the strict limits of justice. On 8th July 1605, a month after Espeleta's murder, they decided that the prisoners should be released; but not without a stain on their characters.

" In the case of Doña Andrea de Cervantes, Doña Juana Gaitan, Doña Catalina de Aguilera, Doña Constanza de Obando, Doña Luisa de Ayala, Doña Isabel de Saavedra, Doña Maria de Arganedo, Doña Mariana Ramírez, Miguel de Cervantes and Don Diego Miranda, arrested, by order of the magistrate Villarroel, by constables Diego Garcia and Francisco Vicente, and in the case of Simón Méndez, lodged in the city jail as a preventive measure pending promulgation of sentence :

" Simón Méndez shall not enter this (the Cervantes') household, nor shall he hold converse in public or in private with this woman (Isabel de Saavedra) ; and Don Diego de Miranda, within fifteen days, shall leave and quit this capital, and he and Doña Mariana Ramírez shall not meet, in public or in private, under penalty of being punished for living in a state of concubinage, and the said Don Diego and Doña Mariana shall pay six ducats for the benefit of the poor and by way of costs ; and Doña Andrea and Doña Juana and the rest shall be released under bond to stay in their own house and not stir from it, and Miguel de Cervantes shall be their surety."

With this sentence the case came to an end, and we know nothing more about it. We have no information when the ban was lifted which condemned all the women in the house, without any distinction between their degrees of innocence in this alleged house of ill-fame, to live the life of cloistered nuns.

It may very well be that it did not last very long, for Villarroel had already achieved his main object. He had managed to distract the attention of anybody who was tempted to pry into the circumstances of Espeleta's murder. He had done so by dint of tearing some handy reputations to tatters.

But it was cruel, as well as unjust, to inflict such wounds upon women who, even if the very worst that was said about them was to be believed, were doing no more than follow the customs of their time.

I have already said that *Fastiginia*, those memoirs of the Portuguese Pinheiro da Veiga, might well be entitled " A Mirror of Loose Morals." Through its pages, amid the record of the extravagance which kept on exhausting the depleted Spanish treasury, scandalous sayings and doings go leaping madly like playful kids amid a flock of staid goats. No reticence restrained anybody's tongue, and little sense of shame tied anybody's hands, among all the people who went for a stroll in the Espolón, or in the gardens which the Marquis of Camarasa threw open to the public; and, if the river Pisuerga ran red, it was not so much because of the nature of the soil through which it flowed on its way to the new capital, as because of the conversation it over-heard when it got there.

Widows sighed for release from their widowhood. Virgins sighed because they had no such estate to bemoan. Even married women sighed for somebody to help them, with the complacent tolerance of their husbands, to meet the high cost of living.

There was the lady who heralded the arrival of her spouse with the contemptuous remark: " Hullo, here comes that cuckold of a husband of mine! " There was the damsel who knew enough about the uses of a chamber-pot to reply, with easy effrontery, to the suitor who asked her for the loan of one: " I'm sorry, but nobody has had a drink out of it yet." And Uruk Bey, the Persian ambassador, who was finally assassinated, left a record of his amorous successes, in which, together with the price he had to pay for every one of them, he set down the name of the fair lady and even, sometimes, other details of less importance for History, which takes no interest in the colour of Court ladies' garters or the number of their beauty-spots.

Husbands, who knew how easily their wives got jewels and other valuables, had to put up with the origin of these trinkets being thrown in their faces, if financial embarrassment, temporary or permanent, ever made them want to turn them into money.

"What," said a certain Doña Maria Tellez to her husband, so Pinheiro reports, "did my jewels ever cost you any money? Six years have I been married to you. Never have you bought me anything, and now you propose to rob me of what God and my mother have bestowed upon me. . . ."

Even in the highest social circles, husbands observed with indifference the costly courtships of their better halves, who might be dear, but were not so to them. "I swear to God," the Count of Siruela once exclaimed, "that I do not know what my wife, the Countess, has to offer to these gallants who woo her. I might undeceive them, and tell them that she has such a flabby pair of thighs that they are not worth a maravedi. And yet there is one of these fellows whose wooing has already cost him fifty thousand ducats."

But there was another husband, a gentleman by pedigree if not in his behaviour, a knight of Montesa, but no knight in his chivalry, who carried interested indifference still further. His wife, mistress of a liberal canon, accepted the wooing of a good-looking youth. The canon complained, and the husband tried to persuade the young man to give up a love affair which was doing such damage to his good name and depriving him of a quiet life. The youth refused, whereupon the husband got the canon to pay for his assassination, and proceeded to run him through in person.

He justified his homicide on the ground that the lover had so much offended "me, my honour, and my family's good name," whereas he had neither honour nor a good name left for the rest of his life. But that did not stop him from walking about the streets of Valladolid, a free man.

In Pinheiro da Veiga's book, embedded in his record of the loose living of the capital, there is also just one mention of the name of Cervantes. He is speaking about a certain lady, one of the prettiest and gayest among those who paraded in the Prado, the Portillo and La Huerta, with their faces veiled but their tongues free, who was married to one Don Lope Garcia de la Torre. She

"stayed up all night, gambling in her own house and losing two or even three hundred ducats, without caring a jot about her husband. If he went to bed early, and happened to call to her to come to bed too, she answered:

"'Shut up and let me play, Lope Garcia, will you? Cervantes, hand me that candlestick, and let's see whether I can make him keep quiet. . . . Señor Lope, so long as I am playing with my own property, leave me alone. It will be time enough for you to complain when I am playing with yours.'"

The chronicler adds on his own account: "The truth was —and women like her were well aware of it, however much they might conceal the fact—that she had no property except her own body; and she lived on it and its snares."

But this Cervantes, mentioned by Pinheiro da Veiga, was certainly not the Miguel de Cervantes who had just given to the world the portentous deeds of *The Ingenuous Knight Don Quixote of La Mancha*.

If the republic of letters had not yet humbled itself to the point of acknowledging him as its leader, he was already recognised as a leading figure in it, and one scarcely fitted, by his grey hairs and his laurels, to run after ladies who sat up all night. He may, perhaps, have frequented places where the filling and emptying of purses was entrusted to the chance of throws of the dice, for that would be a bad habit contracted during his soldiering days. But it is not to be believed that any lady would have treated with such familiarity—which would be humiliating even in the case of a young man with whom she was intimate—a man whose beard was grey, whose maimed arm was his pride, and whose name was haloed with praise.

It must surely have been some other Cervantes; for Miguel must have lacked heart for merry-making or running after ladies, seeing how scurvily Fortune treated him in this city of Valladolid, as she did everywhere else and all through his life.

Amid husbands who turned their honour to their advantage, ladies who sold their honour to buy finery, and pushful, impudent swains, it was poor Miguel de Cervantes on whom Fortune thrust inquiry into his household's comings and goings. It was poor Miguel de Cervantes whom Fortune chose to smirch with a sentence which brought his name and his family into disrepute.

CHAPTER XXV

FURTHER editions of *The Ingenuous Knight Don Quixote of La Mancha* were published in the course of 1605 and the following years. The fame of the book spread far and wide.

Doubtless its success surprised the author himself, unaccustomed as he was to being smiled upon by Fortune. Doubtless he hoped that this success would guide his life into more pleasant paths than those which had led him to the capital of Valladolid and into the clutches of the law.

Miguel watched with delight the triumphant progress of his knight all over the world. It is probable, as I have already said, that when he conceived this character of his, in the form in which he first presented him to the public, he had nothing more in mind than providing pleasant, wholesome entertainment—though his imagination, guided by the hand of genius, led him further than he intended. But, now that Cervantes found his hero so well received by ladies and their lovers, by priests and soldiers, by high and low, he felt fonder of him, as you do of a son who does you credit in word and deed, and whom you come to love not only as a son, but also as an honourable, upright man.

Cervantes brooded over his creation with real affection. He conceived him, in the second part of the book, in more pleasing guise, and lavished all the resources of his imagination and his prose upon him.

Don Quixote was no longer, in his author's mind, merely the mild madman, the luckless adventurer, the bemused butt, the paladin who set lance in rest against bad books.

Now he was to aspire to higher deeds. Now the figure who in body, and perhaps also in mind, had not pretended to be much more than a parody of that squireling of Esquivias, presented himself, when he rode out for the third time, idealised and embellished, because by this time his author had delved down into the soul which he had created and discovered unsuspected treasure there.

Between the first part of the book and the second, there is no difference in masterliness of construction. But there is, I think, a difference in intention. The one may have been intended merely as an agreeable recreation. In the case of the other, the author was now conscious that he was writing a work destined to be immortal.

But between the Ingenuous Knight's second riding-out and his third, other interests, other work, played their part in Cervantes' life. During the early days of the year 1606 the Court went back again to Madrid. Miguel, " a man who wrote and transacted business," according to his sister Andrea's description of him in her evidence during the famous trial at Valladolid, had to follow those who wrote and transacted business: councillors, courtiers and civil servants, successful sycophants of letters and disgruntled detractors of them.

In Madrid Miguel had two friends who might be of service to him, either by giving him commissions to execute or by paying him for his books. One of them was the contractor, Juan de Urbina, and the other the bookseller, Robles.

Cervantes and his family took a house in the Calle de la Magdalena, not far from the centre of Madrid, and within a short walk of the two places which concerned Miguel most :

Robles' bookshop and Cuesta's printing-house. Close by, too, were the monasteries of Mercy and of the Trinity, to which tender memories linked him. In the first his father Rodrigo slept his eternal sleep, and to the second he owed the ending of his slavery in Algiers.

Soon after the family's arrival in Madrid, young Isabel de Saavedra, the victim of the sanctimonious Isabel de Ayala's calumny, met and married a gentleman of mature years, of no great fortune, and of such blameless life that nothing would be known about him but for this contact of his with the Cervantes family. His name was Don Diego Sanz del Aguila, and, after leaving Isabel a child, he died in the odour of sanctity.

The newly married couple went to live in a house near the Calle de Jardines, in the San Luis district. When their daughter, Isabel Sanz, came into the world at the beginning of 1608, Miguel would often abandon a chapter which he had begun, or break off a friendly chat in Robles' bookshop, so that, for the first time in his life, he might feel the soft caressing hand of a child playing with his pointed beard, with its gold now streaked with silver.

Doubtless he had never known the little familiarities of fatherhood during the infancy of his daughter, Isabel de Saavedra. It was only years afterwards that he had taken her into his home, first as a servant, and then recognised her as his daughter. This grandchild of his brightened his hours of disappointment with fresh hopes, sweeter than ever now that they were no longer hopes of his own happiness.

But, scarcely a year after the marriage, his young daughter was left a widow. His grandchild's loss of her father, and also, no doubt, the loss of a good friend of his own—for

Aguila, as a friend of Urbina's, must have been Miguel's friend too, and, besides, Aguila's devotion to Isabel made Miguel look upon him as a son—meant a fresh sorrow for Cervantes.

Isabel, however, younger as she was, does not appear to have taken the death of Don Diego Sanz, a husband scarcely suited to her years, so much to heart as her father. A few months after the death of her first husband, she found a second in the person of one Luis de Molina, a native of Cuenca, and confidential agent of the Italian banker, Carlo Strata.

This Luis de Molina had followed the same path as Cervantes from Italy to Spain, by way of the prisons of Algiers. When he was set free and returned to his fatherland, he may have brought some commission or other to Cervantes on behalf of some captives—if any still survived from the time when he was in Algiers—or, more probably, on behalf of some merchant or shipmaster. In any case, as early as the year 1606 he became on friendly terms with the Cervantes family in Valladolid.

In that city, no doubt, he had not found young Isabel so attractive as Isabel the widow and the heiress. He liked her better now that she was not only free, but also in possession of such a fine dowry as was set forth in the marriage contract: " gowns of silk grogram and plush, of taffeta, of satin, of velvet and of damask; ruffs of Flanders lace, overskirts, jackets and shawls of price; rings of diamonds, rubies, and topazes; earrings with pendants, necklaces, hair ornaments, *agnus dei* and crucifixes of gold and bedsteads of price and worked silver. . . ."

By now six editions of Cervantes' book had appeared,

and a seventh was in preparation in Cuesta's printing-house. It was the seventh in order, but it was the first in importance, since it was probably the only one of them all whose publication was personally supervised by the author.

Cervantes did not regard what Isabel had inherited from her late husband as sufficient dowry for the daughter of a man whose praises were on everybody's lips, the author of a work with such a wide sale. He undertook to pay Luis Molina two thousand ducats, for which his friend Juan de Urbina went surety.

This amount of money was prospective rather than assured. The good reception which the public had given his book was what moved Cervantes to be so generous. Such faith had his equally generous friend Urbina in Miguel's deserved success that, in order to guarantee this dowry, he mortgaged some houses which he owned in the Calle del Prado, some acres of land with a house and garden on the Abroñigal river, and two mills at Tembleque.

The girl-widow, Isabel Saavedra, thus found herself provided with a dowry fit for the daughter of a rich family, thanks to an old husband who died before he began to be a nuisance; to a father who trusted too much to Fortune, because she deigned to smile on him for a moment, after long years when she passed him by with a frown; and to a good man who had a fervent admiration for the creator of the figure of the immortal knight, and was proud to call himself his friend.

Very far away now seemed the years of Isabel Saavedra's straitened circumstances in the house of her mother Anna Franca or Rojas, married to a theatre manager neither very successful nor very prosperous, and the still more unfortunate years when she was bereft of her mother and the man who had sometimes played the father to her. Very far away, too, seemed those days when she was received into the Cervantes family, in the capacity of servant to Doña Magdalena. Miguel's sister, knowing all about her parentage, took her in to help with the house-work, but also for the purpose of educating her so that she might later be accepted, publicly and without shame to anybody, as her brother's daughter.

Now Isabel was the wife of Don Luis de Molina, a man of attractive exterior and enterprising and ambitious turn of mind, who promised to be well able to provide comfort, if not luxury, for his new family. But his very qualities turned into defects, which he sharpened into weapons to wound those to whom he should have shown gratitude, and, among them, Miguel de Cervantes.

Luis Molina lost no time in showing how little capacity he had for gratitude, how much more interested he was in Isabel's dowry than in her person, and how keen a man of business he was. In the receipt in which he acknowledged payment of the dowry handed over to his wife, and in which there was specified, item by item, everything that she brought to their marriage as the heiress of her late husband—it amounted to a total value of 14,753 reales—he was careful to point out that the two thousand ducats promised by Miguel, and guaranteed by Urbina, were not included in the amount received.

Doña Catalina, sometime so indifferent a wife, but now devoted to her elderly husband, and resigned to the quiet life she led in Miguel's home, proved more large-hearted. It was she who stood sponsor at the marriage of this daughter of Cervantes who was no child of her own.

Once upon a time, when he had felt the fetters of Barbary upon him, Cervantes had called devoutly on the Blessed Virgin. Earlier even than that, over the waters of Lepanto he had thought he saw the flash of the Exterminating Angel's sword.

Now, at this period of his life, he could not bring himself to believe that everything ended in littleness and wretchedness here below. Now—if, indeed, the gentle flame of mysticism had not always kept alight in his spirit—he felt desire to draw closer to the Divine, through prayer and penitence, come to birth within him once more. So he joined the " Congregation of Unworthy Servants of the Most Holy Sacrament," founded a few months before by the bare-footed Trinitarian Friar Alonso of the Purification. In the course of the same year, Salas Barbadillo, Espinel, Quevedo and Paravicino also entered this pious fraternity.

About this time, too, an old anxiety came to life again for Cervantes. But it was so easily brought to a happy ending that he might well believe that his days of bitterness were now definitely behind him

Once more, towards the end of 1608, he was summoned, together with his guarantor Don Francisco Suárez Gascó, native of Tarancón, to render those notorious accounts of his tax-gathering in the kingdom of Granada. We may suppose that Miguel was now in a position to pay the 2400 reales which were demanded from him by way of arrears. In any case, this was the end, so many years after their beginning, of the proceedings against the luckless tax-collector.

The monastery of the Trinity, where the " brethren " of the Congregation held their services, was quite close to

Cervantes' house, and Robles' bookshop was not very far away.

These three points marked the corners of the triangle of Miguel's life during 1609: hours of thinking and writing in his sunny study at home; pleasant talks in the book-seller's shop, in the midst of young men who aspired to follow the same path of letters and listened with eager interest to the quiet, polished conversation of this man who had lost the use of his left hand in the now legendary " naval battle," and whose right hand had written the most famous work of the day; and then, when the bells of the Trinitarians summoned to prayer, a general exodus from the bookshop and a quiet walk to the church.

On the way, Miguel would chat with his comrades in the pious congregation and in letters, Salas Barbadillo and Espinel, about far-off days when they were unknown soldiers, and these present days of their greater glory; for by now people pointed them out to one another in the streets and quoted witty passages from their works, stamped on the roll of fame by the printing-press.

As they entered the door of the church, a mystical wave of incense and candle-light advanced to meet them. The door creaked shut behind them, scaring away any sense of sadness over wasted years; and all bitterness, all regret, were left outside, floating in the ashen hues of nightfall. . . .

CHAPTER XXVI

But the peace of these days, serene and uneventful, if not actually happy, was not to last for Miguel de Cervantes.

In the middle of October came the death of his good sister Andrea, who had so often helped him out of her own scanty resources. Miguel repaid all her kindness to him by bearing the expense of his beloved sister's burial in the parish church of Saint Sebastian. Her loss marked the beginning of a new series of troubles in his home.

Luis Molina was not proving such a good husband to Isabel as he had promised to be. He had squandered the property which his wife had inherited, and now, in order to squander them too, he was demanding the two thousand ducats pledged for her dowry. The date fixed for payment was close at hand; and Miguel was given to understand by his son-in-law that negotiation about it was not going to remain within the limits of friendly discussion, but would break those decent bounds and become a matter for lawyers and judges.

Next Miguel's wife, Doña Catalina, after five years of conjugal concord, set off one day without saying a word to anybody, presented herself in the office of Don Baltasar de Ugena, a lawyer from her own home, and drew up a will in favour of her relations in Esquivias. Perhaps it was the gentle influence of the good Doña Andrea which had kept her faithful to her duty to her husband, and, once this link of affection that held her was broken, she felt homesick once more for her native village.

Without stopping to think about her old husband, famous but poor, and how hurt he would be by this action of hers, she made her brother, the priest Don Francisco de Palacios, heir to almost all her property. Of her love for her native village we have proof in the clause in her will in which she gave instructions, " that they should bury her in the tomb of Fernando de Salazar Vozmediano, her father, which is in the choir of the church close to the steps of the high altar, underneath a flagstone." No doubt she believed that, in this way, her soul would remain closer, in the next life, to her family in Esquivias than to her family in Madrid.

To Miguel and his family she left a legacy which was rather one of piety than calculated to increase their fortune : to Miguel himself " the vineyard of Juan grapes on the road to Seseña, which covers some four *aranzadas*[1] . . . with the charge that he shall have four Masses said for the repose of my soul every year, and, after his death, the usufruct of its first fruits for two years by Doña Constanza de Ovando, niece of my said husband. . . . And a piece of land of one *aranzada* which is called El Herrador, for his lifetime, and afterwards it shall revert to my said brother Francisco de Palacios. . . ."

Of any legacy to her step-daughter Isabel there was no mention in Doña Catalina's will; but this may have been due not so much to forgetfulness or *amour-propre* as to her desire that none of her property should fall into the hands of that squanderer of inheritances, Luis Molina of unblessed memory.

[1] An *aranzada* is a measure a little over an acre. (Translator's note.)

This testament of Doña Catalina's, drawn up behind the back of her husband and the head of the family, meant a disappointment for Miguel over what he might well think was due to him for keeping a home together. It was coupled with a fresh disappointment over what he might well think was due to him for his talent and his services.

The Count of Lemos had just been appointed viceroy of Naples. Miguel felt homesick for the years of his youth in the cities of Italy. Once more he drew up a record of his services and applied for an appointment in the kingdom of Naples. But it did him no more good than when, on a similar occasion before, they had told him to " try somewhere else."

The Count of Lemos had as his secretary one Don Juan Ramírez de Arellano, who died before the nobleman set out for Naples, in the early days of August 1608. It was expected that this vacancy would be filled in the person of Diego de Amburcea, a *protégé* of the secretary to the Council of War and Marine, Don Esteban de Ibarra. But the fact that Ibarra was away at the moment on his estates in Biscay, combined with the count's fondness for men of letters, led to the post being given to the author Lupercio Leonardo de Argensola.

In a witty letter written from Madrid to Esteban de Ibarra, his disappointed *protégé*, Diego de Amburcea, referred as follows to the count's grief over Arellano's death and the appointment of Argensola and his brother, together with a retinue of minor poets, to offices under the viceroy of Naples. " His Excellency," he said, " was very sad and depressed for the loss of his secretary, and I do not wonder at it, for he made him a bosom companion."

Then Amburcea goes on:

"Three days after the secretary's death, Señor Don Diego de Ibarra and Señor Bartolomé de Aguilar y Anaya, to whose protection you confided me during your absence, called upon His Excellency and, after paying me any number of compliments, of which I confess myself unworthy, proposed me for the secretary's place. The better to persuade His Excellency, they reminded him that it had been agreed between you and him that he should take me as one of his secretaries to the viceroyalty of Naples, and pointed out that I should be as useful to him in that capacity as in connection with his Presidency of the Indies.

"His Excellency admitted that this was so; but he added that, the very night when his secretary died, a courier was setting out for Aragon, and that he had taken advantage of this to write to Lupercio Leonardo de Argensola, inviting him to come and fill the vacancy; inasmuch as for years he had desired to have him in his service and company, and that he also contemplated taking with him the rector of Villahermosa, Argensola's brother."

Amburcea proceeds to comment, with spiteful but circumspect satire, upon the poetical way in which, given the quality of the two secretaries, the business of the viceroyalty will doubtless be conducted.

"They say that all correspondence will be carried on in verse. How odd! For, God bless my soul, ever since the Deluge, at least, orders have been issued, and business has been conducted, and secretaries have worked, one and all in prose, as being a thing natural, proper and inevitable. . . ."

He might have said so with even better reason two years later. By this time the Count of Lemos, influenced by the Argensolas, had gathered around him a regular court of poets and prose writers: the poet Dr. Mira de Mescua, the dialogist Gabriel de Barrionuevo, the bibliophile Fray

Diego de Arce, Francisco de Ortigosa, Antonio Laredo, and Gabriel Leonardo, Lupercio's son.

Until all these posts were definitely filled, the Count of Lemos' residence and the office of his secretary Leonardo were besieged by petitioners for favours and by claimants for justice. Among them was the man who had lost the use of his left hand for the glory of Spain. Cervantes clutched at this chance of seeing once more, before his eyes closed for ever, those cities of Italy which had charmed him in earlier and happier days, and of bettering his humble estate, now redeemed from sheer poverty by the good offices of Don Quixote and Sancho Panza, but still very far from affluent.

He was given a favourable reception, which encouraged his hopes to run high; but it all ended in fair words and smoke. The Count of Lemos set out for Naples in the middle of the year 1610. If he took with him a bodyguard of prose writers and poets, ready to assault History and plant his banner on high, he also left behind him an army of the disgruntled, ready to pound the citadel of his good name with the mortars of jibe and the battering-rams of satire; and among them were pens as sharp as those of Don Luis de Góngora y Argote and Dr. Suárez de Figueroa.

Don Pedro Fernández de Castro, Count of Lemos, Andrade and Villalba and Marquis of Sarriá, was the son-in-law, nephew and favourite of the all-powerful Duke of Lerma. This meant that, in his expectation of his own advancement and his influence on other people's, he was in the position of heir-apparent. The King's will was wholly under the control of my Lord Duke of Lerma, and it was through Lerma that all favours for himself and his friends

reached the count. Lemos had won Lerma's esteem by
showing him a loyalty, a respect and an affection which
the duke did not get from his own sons, the Duke of Uceda
and the Count of Saldaña, and thus it seemed certain that,
in the course of time, Lemos and nobody else would succeed
the duke as favourite of the King and prime minister of
Spain.

When the duties of his rank left him leisure to let his
imagination roam, the Count of Lemos sought the company
of the Muses, and set his thoughts down in elegant verse.
This taste of his made him a friend of all those who held
converse with Apollo. The disappointment of Miguel's
hopes thus meant for him a two-fold bitterness. He knew
that now he could never reach that *aurea mediocritas* praised
by the Latin poet. He knew also—since it seemed that
the estate of author was the best warrant for sailing the
Mediterranean towards the soft sky of Naples—that his
merits were not judged as high as those of the other poets
and prose-writers who accompanied the new viceroy.

To this chain of disappointments the heaviest link of all
was added for Miguel by the death of the only sister he now
had left in the world. She had assumed the habit of the
Franciscan Third Order a little earlier, and on 11th
October 1610, feeling that the finger of God signalled her
death as not far off, she drew up her will before the notary
Jerónimo López. It was the testament of a poor woman,
who had nothing to leave but a happy memory of her
humble life. In the early days of the next year she surrendered her soul to God. They buried her in the Franciscan
convent, as befitted her poverty.

CHAPTER XXVII

CERVANTES' home sank deeper into the shadows of sad thoughts. Lost voices rang louder in the memories of those who survived than spoken words did in their ears.

Doña Catalina, soon to leave that home herself, sighed for the days of her bygone youth. Constanza, that sweet niece of his who seemed to Miguel the gentle shade of his dead sisters in the silent house, watched her hours and days passing amid melancholy memories and unfulfilled hopes.

Miguel himself no longer had the consolation of other days now distant, when he could feel little Isabel's baby hand stroking his face. Between his home and his son-in-law Molina's lay a long road barred by suspicion, greed and misunderstanding.

Cervantes knew by now that his daughter was married to a selfish, spendthrift husband, whom no sense of decency, no qualms of conscience, restrained if he wanted money to squander. When the hour of his death came, Luis Molina left in rough draft, like a blurred mirror of his conscience, a record of his misdeeds with his wife's and other people's property. Miguel, however, was never to know of this public confession of his son-in-law's.

He was never to know of it in words, but he could tell from acts what he had to expect from Luis Molina. When the definite breach between them came in 1611, Miguel's mind was already prepared for it by bitter hours of unease and anxiety. The time-limit for the payment of the dowry promised by Miguel to his daughter was reached on 28th August and Molina did not wait long afterwards before claiming the two thousand ducats from his father-in-law.

On 17th September he presented himself, with Miguel's written promise to pay the dowry, before the magistrate Fernando Ramírez Farinas and the provincial notary Juan de Campillo, who issued an order for payment and execution. Miguel de Cervantes could not raise the sum demanded, and execution was accordingly directed against his generous friend, the contractor Juan de Urbina. This was an even greater source of bitterness to Cervantes than if the money had come out of his own pocket.

Juan de Urbina handed over 19,000 reales within twenty-four hours of receiving the demand, and promised to pay the balance of three thousand reales within the next few days. Hereupon Molina granted a stay of execution: very generously, so he said himself. Cervantes recompensed Urbina for his ducats with promises and a codicil to his will—in other words, with payment in hope—and the whole matter lapsed into a fresh book-keeping transaction between Urbina and Cervantes' son-in-law.

If this transaction was never cleared up, it was more Molina's fault than the contractor's. Even before proceedings were taken about the dowry, the two of them were involved in an unlucky liquidation in connection with ironworks. All these troubles, together with various other embroilments with men of business and money-lenders, burdened Urbina all his life long, and he left the thread of his affairs hopelessly entangled when he died on 23rd January 1632.

From the negotiations and proceedings over the dowry, it seems to emerge that Cervantes had a right to the usufruct of the house in which his daughter lived, as executor and sole heir of his granddaughter, so long as she was a minor and unmarried. But this right of his never became effective during his lifetime. It was exercised by Molina instead.

Miguel enjoyed no inheritance from his first son-in-law. Even of the immaterial heritage of his granddaughter Isabel, made up of childhood's smiles and childhood's joys, which was so necessary to him to make him forget all his disappointments, all his embitterment, he was now deprived by the separation between the two households.

It was in such circumstances that Cervantes went on writing the second part of his *Ingenuous Knight*, which his public were now demanding for their entertainment, and his publisher on more material grounds. He had also started work on his *Exemplary Tales*. But all his work was in disorder, just like his life. He wrote his pages in fits and starts, and then left them alone for months at a time.

Meanwhile he and his family moved from house to house, as the state of their finances dictated. From the house in the Calle de la Magdalena they moved to another situated behind the College of Our Lady of Loreto; then back again to the Calle de la Magdalena, though to a different house; next to the Calle de Leon, and after that to the Calle del Duque de Alba.

Later on, in connection with his *Adjunct to Parnassus*, Miguel received a missive that reminded him of the sad waste of money for the postage of the indifferent and insulting sonnet which he had received in Valladolid. We learn of still another domicile of his in Madrid from the address on the letter: " To Miguel de Cervantes, in the Calle de las Huertas, opposite the houses where the Prince of Morocco used to lodge."

About this time literary clubs or cenacles, called academies, started to be formed in Madrid. The most important of them, so far as the galaxy of talent that gathered there was concerned, was known as the " Sylvan." We hear of it, among other sources, from Pedro Soto de Rojas, in his *Love's Deceit*: " In the year 1612," he says, " the Sylvan academy was opened in Madrid, so called because it met in the house of Don Francisco de Silva, that man of fine brain and noble heart. . . . The leading writers of Spain then in Madrid attended this academy. . . ."

But the poet Cristóbal de Mesa and the prose-writer Suárez de Figueroa jeered wittily at these conventicles of discord.

> " If some of them formed an academy,
>   There were schism and sect
>   Worse than in England or Bohemy.
>   Some have I seen of these elect
>   Whom needs must they eject,
>   As 'twere a school of heresy. . . ."

So says Mesa, and Suárez de Figueroa writes:

" Some of the fine wits of Madrid discovered recently how much they liked one another, and accordingly they met together in some gentlemen's houses; but these meetings were not a success. The reason was probably that, forgetful of their fine principles, they persisted in writing verses about this, that and the other. Thus were born criticism, meddling, and rivalry, and no little disagreement and difference. Arrogance, presumption and plain speaking reached such a pitch that sometimes they led not only to slights and insults, but even to dangerous quarrels and brawls. . . ."

Lope de Vega, too, despite the fact that he was the acknowledged head of some of these academies, such as the Sylvan,
made fun of the bad temper and the quarrelsomeness of the
academicians. " The academies are full of fury," he writes
to the Duke of Sesa; " in the passage two licentiates pulled
off one another's caps . . ."

This passage would be merely picturesque, if it were
not followed by another which once more links the two
glorious names together—in no straight line of admiration, but in a jagged lightning-flash of jeering jealousy.
" I have read," adds Lope de Vega, " some verses containing
some of the fancies of *the* Cervantes, which seem to me like
badly scrambled eggs."

Miguel also attended this Sylvan academy; but he was
obscured by the immanent shade of the Phœnix of letters.
Perhaps, now that the two of them were growing old,
somebody may have tried to reconcile them. It is even
possible that they were polite to one another's faces.

But on the proud soul of Lope were stamped, with a
red-hot seal, those ironical references to his work which
Miguel de Cervantes had made in the first part of *Don
Quixote*. Even if there had been nothing earlier between
them, this would have sufficed to make Lope eternally
unforgiving towards Miguel. The famous poet, the playwright whom theatre managers besieged, could not understand why, in the chorus of general praise of him, the voice
of this yapping little cur should be raised to mar the
panegyric.

Miguel, for his part, was embittered because his dramatic
works were set aside in favour of somebody else's works,
which—wrongly in this case—he judged inferior to his

215

own. He gives vent to this feeling in his *Adjunct to Parnassus*, to which I have already referred.

> *Pancracio.* " And have you already written any (plays) ? "
> *Miguel.* " I have written six, together with six farces."
> *Pancracio.* " Then why has none of them been staged? "
> *Miguel.* " Because the managers do not run after me, and I am not going to run after them."
> *Pancracio.* " Perhaps they don't know that you have written these plays."
> *Miguel.* " Yes, they do ; but, as they have their own hireling poets, and get on very well with them, they don't need to go gleaning."

Such arrogance, such bitterness on the part of Cervantes could scarcely conduce to sincere friendship. In any event, all this was merely a freshet added to a sleeping pool of unpleasant memories. Tempestuous love-affairs of Lope's with two women of remarkable beauty had found an inconvenient witness in Cervantes, and, in the case of one of them, a commentator cutting in his satire as well.

In his better days, the days of his youth, Miguel had been on friendly terms with the family of the playwright Jerónimo Velázquez, one of whose daughters was married to the actor Cristóbal Calderón. She and Lope made themselves the scandal of the capital by the utter shamelessness with which they flaunted their illicit love. When the erring wife, in response to her family's prayers and threats, broke with Lope, he gave free rein to his invective against his late mistress and her advisers. Doubtless he believed that Miguel, as a friend of the family, was among those who had most strongly influenced the wife to return to her husband.

Even clearer, at least in Lope's opinion, was the part which Miguel had played against him in Seville. In course

216

of a new adventure with another actress, the famous Luján, Lope went to that city, possibly with the intention of keeping their love-affair quiet, but actually with the result of creating a fresh scandal. Then there appeared a sonnet which Lope's suspicion may rightly have attributed to Cervantes' pen, since later critics, with their minds not inflamed with hatred and jealousy, but bathed in the serene light of literary analysis, have fathered this famous composition upon Miguel.

> " ' They say that Lope came.' ' It cannot be.'
> ' As God lives, he passed by where I sat.'
> ' I can't believe it.' ' But, by Christ,
> ' I tell no lie.' ' I say it cannot be.'
> ' By God, you're hard to satisfy.'
> ' A jest, I say.' ' I tell you he came in
> ' By Macarena.' ' And who saw him ? '
> ' I saw him.' ' But he's invisible.'
> ' Invisible, Martin ? There you err ;
> ' For Lope de Vega is a man,
> ' Like you, or me, or Diego Díaz.'
> ' Is he tall ? ' ' Why, yes, about my height.'
> ' Not so tall, then, as his tale—
> ' And that's your fault, his, and his Muse's.' ' "

These and other gibes, some of them really spoken or written by Cervantes, while others of them were only attributed to him by their authors—just as a mischievous boy, before throwing a stone, will hide himself behind the bush that shelters him best, because it is the leafiest—separated the two men of genius for ever. Their physical association at the academies did not suffice to unite them in mind.

They were divided even by the difference in rank which reputation assigned to them. Over that barrier no friendship could pass from one of their hearts to the other.

Lope de Vega lorded it beneath the canopy which enthusiastic dithyrambs wove for him. Miguel, even now that Don Quixote was riding about the world and making people admit that his creator was a paragon of thinkers and writers, went to these gatherings humbly, begging that charity of courtesy and compliment which he craved so much, and of which, all his life long, he went so poor. . . .

CHAPTER XXVIII

IN the year 1613 appeared Cervantes' *Exemplary Tales*, which he dedicated to the absent Count of Lemos.

By now, no doubt, he was schooled by the contempt with which the Duke of Béjar had treated his *Ingenuous Knight*, and by Lemos' utter disregard of his merits when he petitioned the count to take him in his train to Naples. But by now, too, Miguel was surer than before of his own worth.

In his dedication he did not ask for favours, as he had been wont to do. Instead, he proclaimed that he was bestowing a favour by inscribing the count's name in a book which he hoped would prove as famous as his *Don Quixote*.

"Nor do I ask Your Excellency to take this book under your protection, for I know that, if it is not a good one, even though it were placed under the wings of the Hippogriff of Astolfo and in the shade of the Club of Hercules, that would not prevent the Zoilus, the Cynics, the Aretines and the Bernias from flinging the darts of their vituperation at it, without any respect for anybody. I merely beg to inform Your Excellency that I am addressing to you, without comment, twelve tales which, if they had not been fashioned in the workshop of my imagination, might claim their place among the best."

This good opinion which he has of his own work is repeated in his prologue:

"To this I applied my imagination, since thither my inclination led me, the more so as I take leave to claim (which is no more than the truth) that I am the first author to write fiction in the Spanish language, inasmuch as all the many tales which are printed in it are merely translations from foreign languages, whereas these are my own, neither imitations nor pilferings. My mind engendered them, and my pen adorned them. . . ."

In making this claim, Cervantes is scarcely sticking quite closely to the truth—since there are two, at least, of these *Exemplary Tales* which have a foreign physiognomy, if not a foreign accent. But there is no doubt about what he writes earlier:

"One thing I venture to say to you: that, if it could in any way be advanced that the reading of these tales might induce bad desires or thoughts in anybody who read them, I would cut off the hand that wrote them sooner than issue them to the public."

The most interesting thing in this prologue, however, is the portrait which Cervantes paints of himself, physically and intellectually. In his outward appearance, he depicts himself as, by now, toothless and bowed with age; in his inward aspect, as still retaining a juvenile freshness, which is reflected in his zest for creating new characters.

"He whom you see here is of aquiline countenance, with chestnut hair, a brow smooth and high, bright eyes, and a nose hooked, though well-proportioned; a beard of silver, which less than twenty years ago was of gold; a heavy moustache, a small mouth, teeth neither small nor large, for he has but six left and these in bad condition and poorly placed, since they do not correspond with one another; a body between the two extremes, neither tall nor short; a fresh complexion, rather sallow than swarthy; somewhat bowed of shoulder, and none too light on his feet. Such, I say, is the likeness of the author of *Galatea* and *Don Quixote of La Mancha*. . . ."

He goes on:

"After them—the *Exemplary Tales*—if life is left to me, I shall offer you *The Troubles of Persiles and Sigismunda*; and before that, and very shortly, the further adventures of Don Quixote and the further witticisms of Sancho Panza ; and then my *Weeks in the Garden*."

For the copyright in his *Exemplary Tales*, Cervantes received one thousand six hundred reales from Robles the bookseller. This sum may seem small to us to-day, but it was not so bad for those days. As soon as these ingenious, polished *Tales* made their appearance, they followed the same path as their elder brother the *Ingenuous Knight* into the field of fame. Editions succeeded one another, to the total number of six, in the short space of time between their first publication and Cervantes' death.

All fiction hitherto published in the Spanish language had been imported from Italy, and even from Byzantium and Gaul. But, though one or two of these *Exemplary Tales* bore the marks of having come on a journey, most of them had no such foreign origin, but were built up out of material found on the spot, in the street, in the tavern, in the home. Everybody recognised the characters in *The Little Gipsy*, *The Illustrious Fregona*, and *Rinconete* as old friends. Everybody took these characters home to entertain them with their doings and their sayings.

From the time when Miguel's *Exemplary Tales* were published until the time when they were followed by *Journey to Parnassus*, a year elapsed. During this time his faint hopes of gaining some recompense for his assiduous devotion to the Count of Lemos expired one by one. He had no great faith in the protection of the great; but reality itself fell short of his modest illusions.

In the humble homes where he lived in Madrid, Miguel watched the days of his old age passing one by one, in a poverty which was merely relieved by the one thousand six hundred reales earned by his *Tales*. Meanwhile, in Naples, the viceroy snuffed up the incense burned by his secretaries and sycophants at the academy of the " Leisured," founded by the Argensolas. Bartolomé bemoaned the loss of the Count of Gelves, Lemos' brother, in a pompous lament:

> " With thee expired—I make no empty vaunt—
> One whom, with flashing sword in hand,
> Not e'en Alcides' club could daunt . . ."

Or he lauded the skill in the lists of poetry of the viceroy's other brother, the Count of Castro:

> " For you have but to see the fishermen
> At work with patient barque and ready net,
> To soar in thought transcendent.
> How fine a gift it is that ever yet
> Can find, to elevate the minds of men,
> In humble things its instrument ! "

But he sharpened his pen for even loftier dithyrambs when it was a question of singing the praises of his own lord and master:

> " For thee the elements disarm.
> Through thee the sun consents to shine.
> The wind, responsive to thy charm,
> Dies, and the floods, all thine,
> Mount to the clouds, forbearing harm,
> And bring forth flowers in rain benign."

Scant attention was my lord the Count of Lemos likely to pay to somebody or other far away who sent him a collection of tales, but at the same time serenely refused to lick his boots. Why should my lord the count pay any attention to this person, when he had at his command poets who compared him with Jupiter and Atlas?

Apart from Robles the bookseller's ducats, Miguel's dozen of *Exemplary Tales* earned him nothing but some poor, lukewarm praise from the critics of his time. They earned him, in addition, the assurance that Fortune, even if that fickle dame might still be summoned by the shrill voice of an old man, would never be led to his door by the hand of any grandee.

His bitterness because he could find no soft seat in which to rest his weary limbs, amid all the poets and poetasters who prospered under princely patronage, breathes through all the stanzas of his *Journey to Parnassus*. In the learned assembly which makes up the court of Apollo, there is no vacant chair wherein he may sit, and the god says to him :

" ' But if you would escape your plight
' And be at ease, and carefree and content,
' Double your cloak, and sit you down upon it.'
' Easy to see, my lord,' I answered him,
' You do not notice that I have no cloak.'
' Even so,' he said, ' I bid you welcome here ;
' For virtue is a mantle with which poverty
' Can hide its nakedness ; and poverty
' From jealousy is in itself defence.'
I bowed my head to his wise words.
I stayed afoot, for none can find a seat,
Unless it be by favour, or by wealth. . . ."

Out of all of them—Lope de Vega, Mira de Mescua, Góngora, the Argensolas—Miguel de Cervantes was the least favoured. He alone had no cloak to serve him as a seat after the burden and heat of the day, or as a pillow for his dreams. He alone was left afoot among all these loafers on cosy cushions.

About this time, in connection with the beatification of Saint Theresa, a competition in poetry, a Court event, was announced. In this competition there was but one theme: a hymn to be written, in the metre of Garcilaso's *Two Shepherds' Sweet Lament*, in honour of the divine ecstasy of the blessed Sister Theresa of Jesus. The prizes were three: a silver cup, eight yards of camlet, and a pair of silk hose.

The jury consisted of three sprigs of lordly houses, who, no doubt, had inherited talent and taste together with their great names: Don Rodrigo de Castro, son of the Count of Lemos; Don Melchior de Moscoso, son of the Count of Altamira, and Don Francisco Chacón, son of the Count of Casarrubias. Associated with them, to guide their halting steps, was the greatest literary prodigy of his day: Lope de Vega, poet consummate as the Argensolas, and, like them, an inspired artificer of eulogy—though his was more often spoken than written.

But still, just for this once, the enmity which divided the two men of genius drew in its horns. Their sharpness may have been blunted by some hint from higher circles. Be that as it may, one of the prizes was awarded to the composition presented by Miguel, and Lope granted it the honour of reciting it himself.

It would be pleasant to believe that the enmity between Miguel and Lope was quenched from this moment; but their later years serve to give the lie to any such idea. Uncomplimentary to Lope though it may be, it is probably nearer to the truth to imagine that he acted in this way with the deliberate intention of humiliating the old, unfortunate author whose pallid orb had once sought to eclipse the blinding splendour of Lope de Vega.

"Here you may see"—so Lope's thoughts may have run—"the man who once dared to try and supplant me in your taste and your affection. Here he comes humbly to-day to receive a prize at my hands, like any fledgling poetaster. I do not choose to hold his past pretensions against him, and I give you proof of my large-heartedness by taking these poor stanzas of his under my protection. . . ."

We do not know what motive impelled Miguel de Cervantes to dispute for this trophy with young men, who needed some favouring breeze to waft their praises more than he did. It may have been that Miguel needed the silver or the camlet even more than they did. . . .

CHAPTER XXIX

Now came the most painful moment for Cervantes in his life as a writer. Even when the Barbary pirates robbed him of all the reward of his youth, when he saw all his hopes sink beneath the Mediterranean waves, perhaps he did not suffer so much as now, when pirates of another kind on land tried to rob him of the fruits of his old age.

In the prologue to his *Exemplary Tales*, he had already announced the forthcoming appearance of the second volume of *Don Quixote*. He had more than half completed this further instalment of his famous hero's deeds, when there was published in Tarragona a book which bore the title : " *Second Volume of the Ingenuous Knight Don Quixote of La Mancha*, which contains his third riding-out and is the fifth part of his adventures. Written by the Licentiate Alonso Fernández de Avellaneda, native of the town of Tordesillas."

The pirates broke into Cervantes' strong-room and sought to rob him, by anticipation, of the profit which the poor man expected to make out of the second volume of his *Don Quixote*. Worse even than that, just like highway robbers, they beat him up with the cudgels of insinuation and denunciation, and left him, as they hoped, for dead.

In the prologue to Avellaneda's book, Cervantes' prologue to the first part of his *Don Quixote* was branded as " braggart." His prologue to his *Tales* was described as " a piece of impudence and an insult to his readers," and the *Tales* themselves as " more satirical than exemplary."

Avellaneda went on to say that the methods which Cervantes had employed in writing his *Quixote* were not to be admired.

"If I dissent from these methods, it is because his choice of them is an affront to me, and particularly to the man whom the most remote nations so justly applaud, and to whom our own country owes so much, in that for so many years, worthily and tirelessly, he has supplied the theatres of Spain with plays stupendous and innumerable, written with all the art that the public demands, and with all the orthodoxy and purity that are to be expected from a minister of the Holy Office."

This perfectly explicit defence of Lope de Vega seems to indicate that the real author of Avellaneda's book was one of Lope's friends—if, indeed, this friendship was not carried to such a point that it merged into one person and the author was Lope himself.

These angry words might be excusable, on the ground of zeal in defence, if they were not followed by others even more furious still: words flung by the handful, without order or method. Amid them, however, jealousy emerges like the refrain of a song. Doubtless the author's heart was so full of it that it had to come out on the point of his pen.

"Besides, Miguel de Cervantes is now as old as the castle of San Cervantes, and, because of his years, so dissatisfied that he dislikes everything and everybody, and as a result he has so few friends that, when he wants to adorn his book with high-sounding sonnets, he has to attribute them, as he admits himself, to Prester John of the Indies and the Emperor of Trebizond, doubtless because he cannot find a single man in all Spain who would demean himself by speaking his name. . . .

"Let him content himself with his *Galatea* and his prose plays, which have the advantage over his novels that they do not actually bore us. Saint Thomas (*Secundae Secundae quaestio* 36) teaches that envy does no harm to anybody but oneself. . . . But let us excuse the faults of his *First Part*, on the ground that it was written within the walls of a prison, and so it could not fail to emerge stamped with the prison taint, or be anything else but querulous, vindictive, impatient and choleric. . . ."

This other passage also smacks of defence of Lope, since it turns ridicule of borrowed eulogies back upon Cervantes, though not in his own witty way of inventing pompous, non-existent praises of his books. What is delicate irony in the case of Cervantes becomes mere coarse insult in the case of his detractor.

The passage smacks, too, of the tribunal of the Holy Office to which Lope now belonged. It was too proud to meet wit with wit and satire with satire; but it was quite ready to use flaming language—since in this case it could not use the stake—to blast the reputation of the man who had dared to stray, however little, from singing its praises and accepting its guardianship of conscience.

We cannot, therefore, regard critics who blame the paternity of the false *Quixote* upon Lope de Vega as unduly daring, though we cannot be certain that he actually conceived and wrote it himself.

With still less reason has this book—this jackdaw which, by taking the name of the glorious crazy Knight, hoped to adorn itself with the plumage of a bird of paradise—been attributed to the mediocre wits of more or less witty mediocrities, such as Doctor Blanco de Paz, Cervantes' bitter and envious enemy in the prisons of Algiers; Father Aliaga, Philip III's confessor; the Jacobin friar Alonso Fernández, the Valencian Juan José Martí, already the continuator of *The Roguish Guzmán de Alfarache*; or that bad Aragonese poet, Alonso Lamberto.

228

Names of the highest literary standing have also been dragged in, such as those of Tirso de Molina, Ruiz de Alarcón, and Bartolomé Leonardo de Argensola. Indeed, critics are not lacking, like the great English Cervantist Fitzmaurice Kelly, who would have us believe that it was Cervantes himself who issued this faked second part to the public, as a forerunner of the real one which, at the same time, would provide a touchstone of its excellence.

None of the persons mentioned above—with the exception of Blanco de Paz and Lope de Vega himself—had any personal grounds for disliking Cervantes and attacking him and his work in such harsh terms as are to be found in the prologue to the book signed by Avellaneda. The friar who was a captive with Cervantes in Algiers has left us no other fruits of his inconspicuous brain-power which entitle us to infer that this second part of *Don Quixote* was any work of his; and besides, he was so old that he could scarcely hold a pen.

Almost all those to whom the conception and birth of this monstrosity have been attributed were clerics. But this is a deduction from its prologue, which took the form of a dreary sermon. It is not a deduction from the true *Don Quixote*. If that work had really offended the Church, she had learned men at her command who could have adorned its author with a *sambenito* and consigned him and it to the flames.

By a process of exhaustion, Lope de Vega himself remains as the most likely author, or at least instigator, of this literary crime.

We need not assume that Lope was so completely lacking in human virtues as Don Ramón Leon Mainez depicts him:

" perfidious, selfish, revengeful, haughty, contemptuous, proud in the extreme, infatuated with himself. . . ." Since his premature judgment had been given the lie by *Don Quixote's* success, he may well have felt mortified at appearing in the role of a false prophet, and sought to cry quits by fathering a fake. He may have regarded this as no more than a little joke between literary colleagues.

In any case it is difficult to explain away those circumstantial words which I have already quoted: " . . . (Cervantes') *choice of them is an affront to me, and particularly to the man whom the most remote nations so justly applaud, and to whom our own country owes so much*, in that for so many years, worthily and tirelessly, he has supplied the theatres of Spain with plays stupendous and innumerable."

Moreover, if there was any satire in the first part of *Don Quixote* that was not purely objective, it was that which Cervantes directed against Lope's mannered novels and the eulogies of himself in verse with which he prefaced them: eulogies which sheltered under the wings of proud eagles, but, as a matter of fact, came out of no other nest than Lope's own imagination. For this reason, Lope regarded himself as being the target both of the first part and of the entire book. His supporters believed that Cervantes' work as a whole was a battering-ram constructed to demolish their idol's reputation.

" An affront to me, and particularly to the man whom . . ." reads like a puerile distinction with which the author, disguising himself as a warm-hearted and disinterested champion, tried to throw anybody seeking to identify him off the scent. Nobody was affronted—if good-humoured satire is to be regarded as an affront—except Lope. The "me" and "the man whom" look very much like one and the same person. If Lope was merely the instigator of the work, its actual writer identified himself so completely with the affronted party that he felt the affront just as though it had hurt him in his own person and his own dignity.

In the sonnets and mottoes which appeared on the title-pages of their books, Lope de Vega and Cervantes mutually disputed one another's title to be regarded as the one and only author: Lope, in his *Pilgrim*, with the device: " *Velis, nolis, Invidia, aut unicus aut peregrinus* "; and Cervantes, in his *Don Quixote*, through the mouthpiece of Amadis of Gaul:

> " You shall have high renown for worth,
> Your fatherland shall be of all the first,
> You learned author, in this world unique and sole."

But this latter may be read as a piece of wry humour which Cervantes applies to himself; whereas, in the case of Lope, the motto of his book is an evident piece of arrogance.

Besides, apart from all this, other compositions, more suitable for word of mouth than for print, came into circulation about this time, either from Lope's own hand or that of some fervent partisan of his and enemy of Cervantes. Among them was that scurrilous sonnet which was attributed to Lope, doubtless for the very good reason that it looked like his. Later, when Góngora had said just what he thought about it and the opposite camp could exhibit it as a reproach to Lope, the ill will of its instigators actually attributed it to Cervantes himself. Here is what Lope said, or was supposed to have said:

231

" I may not know one thing from another,
  Or whether you, Cervantes, are this or t'other.
  But this I say: Lope's Apollo, and you
  His carriage-horse, and pig-like, too.
  Lest you should ever write, a thing like you,
  'Twas Heaven's will to maim you at Corfu.
  You spoke, you ox, but all you said was ' Moo.'
  So honour Lope, churl, or look to you.
  For he's the sun, and, if he's wrath, there's rain.
  And as for you and your *Don Quixote* vain,
  He's only fit for wrapping grocery,
  Or better still on dunghill be,
  Or best of all in privy."

To anyone who has found delight over and over again in Cervantes' prose and Lope de Vega's verse, it is painful to think that the one of them should ever have been so vilely insulting, or the other of them ever have been a target for such insults. One would like to believe that this sonnet did not come from the same pen that wrote " To my solitudes I go," or " Poor little barque of mine." But then we remember how Lope was sued for libelling some actors. By dint of his own scurrility, he breaks down the doubt which separates these compositions in our minds, and we are driven to believe that the name of Lope covers one and all of them.

When Lope de Vega cited the writers and other men of merit of his time in his *Jerusalem Conquered*, he left out Miguel de Cervantes. He never mentioned that name except to vilify it. This was at a period when Cervantes' reputation as the foremost of Spanish novelists had spread so widely that his name had already become proverbial in conversation and in the verse and prose of the most renowned writers of the day.

> " That strangest of all love tales
> Which Cervantes wrote,"

says Calderón in his *House with Two Doors*; and, in his *Realms of Sunset*, he adds:

> " My love is so romantic
> That Cervantes wrote it for me."

And Quevedo, in his *Perinola*, advises Montalván to " leave fiction to Cervantes."

It was only Lope de Vega who disregarded his genius, or deliberately closed his eyes lest he should see its splendour. It was only Lope who felt himself offended by the first part of *Don Quixote*. It was only in his interests, only as a product of his ill will, that this faked second part could have been written. It contains much beauty; but it is all overshadowed by the cloud of that sinister prologue. . . . It is a thousand pities that the clear crystal of one's admiration for Lope de Vega should be smirched and shattered by the thought of such a thing.

CHAPTER XXX

It's an ill wind that blows no good. The work signed by Avellaneda proved a springboard for Cervantes which enabled him to outleap even his own reputation and aspire to the stars.

It was this that acted as a stimulus for the final chapters of his *Don Quixote*, which accomplish the difficult feat of surpassing the earlier ones in inventiveness and beauty of expression.

When Cervantes began his great work in prison in Seville, he may have hesitated a good deal over the pages which contained his prologue; but he must have hesitated a thousand times more over the pages which contained the text. He felt himself torn between conflicting desires, and, amid them all, the outline of his work wavered like a feather in an eddy.

He had not set hand to his task with any loftier aspiration than that of providing pleasant entertainment and tilting against bad books. But now, when he looked back upon his own work from a distance, and compared it with that of the knock-kneed writers who presumed to stand in his way, he could measure and comprehend its greatness.

Miguel started writing his *Second Part of the Ingenuous Knight Don Quixote of La Mancha* with the consciousness that it was a work of genius. Now that he had it half written, when he stumbled upon Avellaneda's offspring, he found his own *Don Quixote* so vastly different from the piratical one that he felt like an eagle flying in the blue of

234

Heaven, with only its shadow dragging itself across broken ground far below.

The *Don Quixote* engendered in Tordesillas and born in Tarragona had at first filled Miguel's heart with bitterness. But, as the days passed, he came to look upon it without hatred, because he owed to it the fact that, once and for all, he believed in his own genius and in the immortality of his own work.

For this reason, and also for the reason that Miguel de Cervantes' pen could not descend to the level of vituperation of Avellaneda's prologue, when the *Second Part of the Ingenuous Knight Don Quixote of La Mancha* was given to the world at the end of 1615, its title-page ignored all baseness, all littleness, and soared into serener skies.

" For in truth I cannot give you this satisfaction," he says to the reader who may expect him to repay insult by insult,

" because, whereas affront awakens anger in the humblest of breasts, my own suffers exception from this rule. . . . The only thing that still hurts me is that I should be reproached with being an old man and a maimed one, as though it were within my power to stay the flight of time, or as though I had lost the use of my hand in some tavern brawl. . . . It has hurt me also that I should be called envious, and that, as though I did not know it already, I should be instructed in what envy means ; whereas, so far as the two of us are concerned, I recognise, on my part, nothing but what is blessed, noble and well intentioned."

And Cervantes ends this passage with heartfelt praise of the man who had defamed him, or at least been instrumental in reviling him :

". . . And if he says what he appears to say to the contrary, he is utterly mistaken ; for I venerate his genius, and I admire his works and his consistently virtuous life. . . ."

For his frank contempt, Cervantes repaid Lope de Vega with a public profession of admiration. He even went so far as to throw the veil of those generous words of his—" I admire his works and *his consistently virtuous life*"—over the shamelessness with which Lope, scorning the obstacle of his cloth, had transferred the laxity of his life as a layman into his life as a priest.

Before he offered the public this work of his, whose prologue in itself foreshadowed its greatness, Cervantes published a volume of plays. They were those to which he had already referred in his *Adjunct to Parnassus*. As they had never been staged, " because managers did not run after him, and he was not going to run after them," he had decided to publish them in book form, " so that what should take place quickly may be observed at leisure."

He was not much more fortunate with booksellers than he had been with theatre managers. He had to make the rounds, with his manuscript under his arm, searching for a publisher—largely because, unlike so many authors of his own time and of all times, he depreciated the worth of his own wares:

> " I, who sweat and burn the midnight oil,
>   To give myself the poet's grace
>   That Heaven denied me . . ."

In his prologue to this volume of plays, he tells the story of his efforts to get them staged or printed.

" Some years ago, I returned to my former pastime, and, imagining that these were still the years when my praises were being sung, I wrote a few plays. But I found no birds in the nests of yester-year; in other words, I found no manager who came and asked me for these plays, though they all knew that I had written them; and so

I flung them into a drawer and consecrated and ordained them to perpetual silence. At that time, a bookseller told me that he would have bought them from me, if he had not heard from a leading manager that of my prose much was to be expected, but of my verse nothing whatever. . . .

" I grew weary of them, and sold them to this same bookseller, who has printed them as I present them to you now. He has paid me a fair price for them ; and I get my money easily, without having to bother about the whims and fancies of actors and actresses."

This serenity with which he accepts other people's opinion of his work extends, in this same prologue, to his own opinion of other people's work—even that of his none too good friend Lope :

" I had other things to occupy me. I laid my pen aside and abandoned playwriting. Then came the reign in the theatre of that prodigy of Nature, the great Lope de Vega, who possessed himself of the dramatic monarchy, subjected all actors to his jurisdiction, and filled the whole world with his own felicitous and well-devised plays."

The bookseller who, after depreciating Cervantes' wares on the strength of other people's opinions, finally took them was Juan de Villaroel. We do not know, however, what amount of money it was that Miguel got so "easily."

This volume of plays included : *The Spanish Gallant, The Lucky Ruffian, The Great Sultana, Pedro de Urdemalas, The Labyrinth of Love,* and *The Mistress,* all mentioned in the prologue to his *Adjunct to Parnassus* ; together with two others, *The Usages of Algiers* and *The House of Jealousy,* which were reprints or revisions from his earlier period— the time when " his praises were sung " as a dramatic author, and his works were staged " without anybody throwing cucumbers or anything else."

237

In his dedication of this book to the Count of Lemos, Cervantes informed him about his prospective works; but it was no longer with that youthfulness of mind, that sense of assurance in his own powers, which he displayed in the prologues to his novels. Every passing day weighed more heavily on his shoulders, bowed by the burden of all his troubles.

> "*Don Quixote of La Mancha* has set spurs to his second part to go and kiss Your Excellency's feet. . . . Then will come the great *Persiles*, next *Weeks in the Garden*, and finally the second part of *Galatea, if my old shoulders can carry all this charge.*"

In this prologue of his, Cervantes betrayed no resentment against the Count of Lemos on account of his disappointment over his frustrate journey to Italy; and, inasmuch as from time to time he received gifts from the count—as he did from Cardinal-Archbishop Sandoval y Rojas—which relieved his ailing and comfortless old age, he continued to send all the fruits of his genius to kiss the count's feet.

While he was producing the last and the most mature of these fruits, during the years 1614 and 1615, an embassy from the King of France arrived at the Spanish Court to conclude marriage contracts between the Houses of Bourbon and Austria. Louis XIII of France was to marry the Spanish Infanta, Anne of Austria, and the Prince of Asturias, afterwards Philip IV, was to marry Isabelle of France, daughter of Henri IV. The French envoy reached Madrid on 15th February 1615, when *Don Quixote of La Mancha* had already set spurs to his mount to go and kiss my lord the Count of Lemos' feet and fill the hearts of all lovers of good books with delight.

But the book was still in the censors' hands. One of them was the Licentiate Márquez de Torres, chaplain to Archbishop Sandoval, Cervantes' patron. This good Cardinal was *persona grata* at the Spanish Court and the French ambassador went to call upon him. When the Cardinal, accompanied by his chaplain, went to return the ambassador's visit, the conversation turned, among other things, on art and literature, of which the ambassador and his suite, like all friends of that good patron of letters, the late French king, were great admirers.

The name of that unlucky genius, whose latest and greatest work Márquez de Torres was at the moment censoring, cropped up in the course of the conversation. De Torres has left us a record of the incident and of the praises which were poured out on the absent head of Miguel de Cervantes like a baptism of immortality.

"On 25th February 1615, the illustrious Señor Don Bernardo Sandoval y Rojas, Cardinal-Archbishop of Toledo, went to return the visit paid to him by the Ambassador of France, who had come to discuss matters touching the marriages between his princes and those of Spain. Several of the French gentlemen accompanying the ambassador, as courteous as they were admirers and lovers of good literature, approached me and my lord the Cardinal's other chaplains, desirous to know what Spanish books were best worth reading at the moment.

"I happened to mention the work which I was just censoring, and they no sooner heard the name of Miguel de Cervantes that they all started talking about him, saying what admiration there was, both in France and in the neighbouring kingdoms, for his works *Galatea*—which some of them knew almost by heart—the first part of the book to which I had referred, and the *Tales*. They questioned me closely about his age, profession, quality and fortune. I was obliged to say that he was old, a soldier, a gentleman, and poor. Whereupon one of them inquired seriously:

" 'Then such a man is not maintained in comfort in Spain out of the public funds ? '

" One of the other gentlemen caught up this train of thought very quickly and said :

" 'If it be necessity that has compelled him to write, please God that he may never have abundance, so that, poor himself, he may continue to enrich the whole world with his works.' "

It is pleasant to reflect that the Licentiate Márquez de Torres kept his word to his new friends and took them to see that genius who was " old, a gentleman, and poor." It was, so to speak, an embassy from the elder branch, a burgeoning of sweet flowers of admiration and affection ; an embassy which the prose-writers of the Court of France sent this poet and prose-writer of Spain.

By now Cervantes had moved from his house in the Calle de Las Huertas, " opposite the houses where the Prince of Morocco used to lodge," to his last resting-place in life, the house in the Calle de Leon, which belonged to the priest Martínez Marcilla.

He had been told by the censor Márquez that a company of his good friends of France were coming to see him, and when they arrived he went to the door of his house to meet them. He walked on gouty feet, dragging them clumsily ; but in his left hand, for the first time since the days of Lepanto, he felt a gentle tremor of life, as though his emotion were turning into fresh sap.

Cervantes' house had one large room, lit by the light of the setting sun, like a symbol of the glory that had come to him now that his own day was almost done. Here he courteously offered the most comfortable chair, the one in which he sat to work, to the most distinguished of his foreign visitors.

CERVANTES MAKES HIS WILL

His guests, grouped round the glorious old man, drank in every word he said and registered everything he did in their minds, so that they might make a welcome present of their memories to their friends at the French Court who had not had the honour of listening to Miguel de Cervantes. In response to their request he told them all about the work that he planned for the morrow and his luckless labours of yester-year. Amid their expectant silence his quiet voice spoke:

" One day, in the prisons of Algiers . . . "

And the sun, shining through the open window, kissed his feet, while from the next room came a soft murmur of women's voices praying or speaking softly . . .

CHAPTER XXXI

IN the middle of November, the second part of Cervantes' eagerly awaited *The Ingenuous Knight Don Quixote of La Mancha* was placed on sale. It followed the same path of swift success as the first part, and within a short time surpassed it in number of editions, while the book engendered at Tordesillas sank into oblivion.

In his dedication to the Count of Lemos, Miguel foreshadowed the publication of *The Troubles of Persiles and Sigismunda* " within the next four months," and soon after this period had elapsed he fulfilled his promise.

About his life during this period we have no more information than that which he gives us himself in the prologue to this last book of his. Afflicted by gout and dropsy, he sometimes sought relief in change of air, in the same way as a bedridden patient seeks relief in change of attitude, and just as fruitlessly. On several occasions he made the journey from Madrid to Esquivias. It was in the course of one of these excursions that he met the " sparrow student " whom he immortalised in the prologue to his *Persiles*.

" It so happened, dearest of readers, that while two friends of mine and myself were on our way back from the famous place of Esquivias—famous for a thousand reasons, one of which is its illustrious families and another its illustrious wines—I heard somebody riding hard behind me, who, to all appearance, was eager to overtake us, and went so far as to show it by shouting to us not to spur so fast. We waited for him, and riding upon a donkey came a sparrow student; for he was dressed all over in brown—leggings, round shoes, sword-scabbard, and vandyke collar with tassels. The truth is that it had no more than two left, for the collar kept on slipping to one side, and he had all the ado in the world to straighten it. He came up with us, and said:

" ' You gentlemen must be hurrying after some office or benefice in the capital, where are His Excellency of Toledo and His Majesty—nothing less than that, judging by the speed at which you ride, for in truth my donkey has been hailed victor in a race many a time.'

" To which one of my companions replied:

" ' Señor Miguel de Cervantes' horse is to blame, for it is something long-stepped.'

" No sooner had the student heard the name of Cervantes than he dismounted, letting his saddle-bag fall one way and his cloak-bag the other—for he travelled with all this paraphernalia—hurried over to me, seized me by the left hand, and said: ·

" ' So you are he—that man, maimed but whole, that most famous of all men, that witty writer, that joy of the Muses! '

" Hearing all this singing of my praises within so brief a space, I felt that it would be discourteous not to reply to it; and so, putting my arm round his neck—which nearly made him lose his collar once and for all—I said to him:

" ' That is an error into which many misguided admirers of mine have fallen. I am Cervantes, Señor, but I am not the joy of the Muses, or any of the other trifles that you mention. Get hold of your donkey again, and mount it, and let us talk together for the little of the way that is left us.'

" So this good student did, and we held our reins something tighter, and went on our way at a leisurely pace. On the way there was talk of my illness, and the good student despaired of me on the spot, saying:

" ' This illness of yours is dropsy, and not all the water of the Ocean will cure it, no matter how sweetly you may drink it. Be measured in your drinking, Señor Cervantes; but do not fail to eat, and you will be cured, without any other medicine.'

" ' So many have told me,' I replied, ' but I might as well give up drinking altogether with a good will, as though I were born for nothing else. My life is drawing to a close, and as my pulse ebbs away—which, at the rate it is going, will finish its career next

Sunday—so I shall be done with life. You have made my acquaintance in the nick of time, but I have none left to show you my gratitude for the kindness you have shown me.'

" With this we came to the Toledo bridge, and he took leave of us to enter the city by the Segovia bridge. Of what he said about me fame will take care; but my friends will be as glad to repeat it as I to listen to it. I turned back to embrace him, he turned back towards me again, he spurred his donkey, and he left me as much upset as he nearly was riding that donkey of his.

" He had given me a fine opportunity to write nice things about him; but all times are not alike. A time may come, perhaps, when this broken thread will be knotted together again, and I may say what I cannot say here and what I feel I should say.

" Good-bye to thanks, good-bye to compliments, good-bye to good friends. For I am dying. May I meet you all again soon, happy in the next life! "

It is a marvel of sad humour, of cheerful resignation, this passage of him. Even if this one short work were the sole product of his pen, it would entitle him to fame as one of the most human and warm-hearted of authors, and one of the most limpid of stylists, among all the writers of the world.

We read it with a sense of troubled tenderness. We see him in our minds' eyes with all that bitter-sweet realism with which he depicts himself: old and bowed down by all his troubles of body and mind, receiving the caresses of popularity with a sad smile, whether they come to him in the ceremonious guise of foreign ambassadors, or in the dishevelled, talkative and enthusiastic figure of an itinerant student.

The sun of all this last winter of his shone wanly and as though it were in a hurry to set. Miguel felt its feeble warmth on his numbed limbs with gratitude, but with no illusions that he could stay it in its course. He knew already that his end was approaching, so rapidly that he could not look beyond " next Sunday ; " but still he forced himself to smile. Nevertheless, at the end his voice broke in a stifled sob : " Good-bye to thanks; good-bye to compliments; good-bye to good friends. . . ."

On two other occasions, either of them likely to be the last time he would take up his pen, he showed himself, in graceful, gentle words, resigned to the inevitable. One occasion was when he penned the dedication of his *Persiles* ; the other, when he replied to that other patron of his, Archbishop Sandoval, who had sent—doubtless with his accustomed gift—to inquire for him.

" Yesterday they gave me Extreme Unction," he says in his dedication to Lemos, " and to-day I am writing this. My time is short, my hopes are waning, my pains are increasing; but still life prevails over any desire that I have to live . . ."

And to the Cardinal, a few days earlier, he wrote :

" If the ill from which I suffer could have any remedy, it should surely find one in the repeated proofs of favour and protection which I receive from your illustrious self; but, in fact, it is getting so much worse that I believe it will make an end of me, though not of my gratitude. . . ."

From the last days of March, his illness kept him confined to bed. Ended were his rides to Esquivias ; ended his short walks to Juan de Villaroel's and Robles' bookshops, where he listened to the gossip of tale-tellers or let his own words fall in soft, fertilising rain upon young brains.

Sitting up in bed, he gazed with hazy eyes into that infinite to-morrow, while he fought for breath and against the horror of eternal silence. Beside him were his niece

Constanza de Ovando, sole brightness of his last years, and that wife of his who had failed to understand him, now sobbing with repentance, with regret for her old love, and with grief over the lonely days before her.

The priest Marcilla, friend and patron of Cervantes, came to his bedside to keep up his spirits with pleasant gossip, and fortify his hopes by bidding him die well. His friend's words came to Miguel's ears; but the rough edge of the priest's exhortations, which combined threats of Hell with promises of Heaven, did not rasp the serenity of his thoughts; and he smiled gently, but undeceived, when they spoke to him of earthly hopes.

"Let God's will be done," he said in his farewell letters to the Cardinal and the Count, and to his family's comfortings he made the same reply.

His eyes kept straying too, towards the half-closed door, through which, at any moment, might come that dear daughter of his, for whose sorrows he was suffering now, and whose tenderness had consoled him in earlier days of his own sorrows. He waited from hour to hour, anxiously wondering which of his two expected visitors would come first, and whether that other awful visitor, who was drawing near so fast, would close his eyes before he could raise them to look upon that beloved face. . . .

He waited from hour to hour; but his daughter never came.

On the second day of April he entered the Third Order of Saint Francis. To this order his two dead sisters had belonged, and in it his wife and his good friend Marcilla had made their profession. It may have been the counsels of the priest, anxious to guide him into heavenly paths, which induced him to assume the habit of the Third Order. Or it may have been the example of those who called to him in voices which he alone could hear.

A few days later, on the 18th, he received Extreme Unction. It was on the 19th that he wrote to the Count of Lemos and told him so with gentle resignation and sweet serenity.

Four more days passed in the room in the priest Martínez Marcilla's house where lay that " old soldier, a gentleman and poor," Miguel de Cervantes Saavedra. Then sounded a stifled sigh; hushed, urgent voices; a swish of hurrying skirts. . . . An endless moment of silence, and, last of all, a bitter burst of shrill lamentation. . . .

Marcilla the priest came to that house of mourning to find the body of his old friend lying still, with his head drooping forward on his breast, and his lofty, marble brow bathed by the light of sunset. At the bedside, Constanza de Ovando and Catalina Salazar de Cervantes mingled their sobs and their prayers. Over the lifeless body Martínez Marcilla stretched forth his arm. It was with his own eyes dim with tears, his own lips trembling, his own voice breaking into a sob, that he murmured:

" Rest in peace for ever and ever ! . . . Amen ! "

CHAPTER XXXII

THEY gave his body sepulture in the monastery of the Trinitarians, near the house where he died.

No Grandees came to his burial, nor did the most famous writers of the day chant his praises over his grave. He was born poor, he lived without ease, and he died with no wealth to bequeath to his family. He left them nothing but the glory of his name, and this so badly dealt with by his contemporaries that it could not serve them for pride, any more than it had served him to relieve his poverty.

He was not lauded either in life or in death by the fashioners of fame, by those who grant credentials as a fine writer in exchange for community singing of their own praises. But his work was not swept away by Time, like that of so many who refused to believe in his genius.

It was on its own merits that it sank its roots deep into Fame, and spread its splendid foliage over all the world. In Miguel's own time, only the lowly could afford to appreciate the racy entertainment of his tales. And so could foreigners; for they, too, need not be afraid lest his well-earned fame should obscure established reputations, some of them won by hard work, and others of them bought by paid eulogy.

Even after Cervantes' death, the envy and the lack of understanding of those who had refused to recognise him and his genius in his lifetime pursued him.

The poet Villegas declares in his *Erotics* that he must conquer Helicon " better than that bad poet Cervantes." And Cristóbal Suárez de Figueroa, in his dialogues entitled *The Traveller*, proclaims Cervantes the author of his own misfortunes, a poet of competition verse, and a writer of plays fit only to be staged in the valley of Jehosaphat.

But there was an almost unknown poet who was moved by Miguel's burial as a member of the Third Order, with his face uncovered, to write this epitaph, full of fine fervour :

> " Wayfarer : the pilgrim
> Cervantes here lies buried.
> Earth takes back his body ;
> His name lives on divine.
> His race at length is run,
> But for his fame, and for his works,
> There is no death. And so it was
> That, passing from this life
> Into the life beyond,
> He went frank-countenanced."

Only the lowly understood him and praised him, because in his work, like Don Quixote tilting at the windmills, he set lance in rest against false greatness; and also because, like his own hero, he was sad and sorry to the end.

At the last, he came to seek the hospitality of eternity in a Trinitarian monastery. So humbly did he ask for repose that they hid him away in an obscure corner where his poor tired bones would not be in the way. He was despised and belittled in death, as he had gone through life belittled and despised.

Just as his own humility and other people's indifference

249

left him one of the anonymous mass in his lifetime, so in death other people's indifference and his own humility, which lasted beyond the grave, huddled away his bones among the nameless dead. To-day no man may tell which are his bones, or even in what corner of that church they rest . . .

INDEX OF NAMES

Acuaviva, Pontifical delegate, 12, 16

Aguilar y Anaya, Bartolomé de, 208

Aguilera, Doña Catalina de, 191

Alarcón, Jerónima,

Alba, Duke of, 90–1, 115–6

Alcalá, Duke of, 132

Alcazaba, Hermit of, 158

Alexandria, Viceroy of, 25

Ali Pasha, 19, 25

Aliaga, Father, 228

Altamira, Count of, 224

Álvarez, Mateo, 158

Álvarez de Toledo, Fernando, 93

Aluch Ali (Uchali), 33–4, 36, 64

Amburcea, Diego de, 207–8

Anastro, Gaspar de, 149

Angulo, Silvestre, 157–8

Apollo, 223, 232

Aragonés, Alonso, 74–5, 85

Arce, Father Diego de, 208–9

Arganedo, Doña Maria de, 191

Argensola, Gabriel Leonardo de, 209

Argensola, Lupercio Leonardo de, 207–9, 223–4

Arguijo, Juan de, 132, 171

Ariño, 154

Aristotle, 169

Arnaute Mami, 45–6, 49–50, 57

Arzón, Marco Tulio, 159

Atlas, 223

Austria, Anne of (wife of Philip II), 92

Austria, Infanta, Anne of, 238

Austria, Don John of, 20, 24–5, 29–30, 33–7, 41, 47, 51, 54–5, 90, 112, 127, 152

Austria, House of, 174, 238

Avellaneda, Alonso Fernández de, 87, 226–31, 234–5, 242

Ávila, Sancho de, 92–3

Ayala, Doña Isabel de, 176, 186–7, 188–91, 199

Ayamonte, Marquis of, 172

Barahona de Soto, Luis, 108

Barbarigo, Venetian admiral, 25

Barbarossa, son of, 34

Barrionuevo, Gabriel, 208

Béjar, Duke of, 171–3, 219

Bella, Father Antonio de la, 79–80

Beltrán de Salto, Captain, 56

Benavides, Diego de, 86

Benito, Nicolás, 138

Berceo, Gonzalo de, 35

Biedma, Pedro de, 84

Blanco de Paz, Father, 75–6, 79, 84–5, 228–9

Borja, Francisco de, 162

Bourbon, House of, 238

Bragadino, 22

Cabrera de Córdoba, Luis, 54

Cáceres, Father Antonio de, 162

Calderón de la Barca, 233

Calderón, Cristóbal, 216

Caliope, 170

Calvin, 174

Camoens, 135

Campillo, Juan de, 212

Camporredondo, Francisco, 183

"Captive, the" (character in Don Quixote), 33–4, 36–8, 69–70

Caro, Rodrigo, 132

Carpio, Marquis of, 115

Carranza, Archbishop Bartolomé de, 40

Casarrubias, Count of, 224

Castañeda, Ensign, 53, 56

Castellanos, Ensign Diego de, 59, 76, 85

Castro, Count of, 222

Castro, Miguel de, 40

Castro, Rodrigo de, 224

Castro del Río, Sacristan of, 122–3

Castroverde, Augustinian monk, 165

Caur Ali, 49

Cervantes, Andrea de (Miguel's sister), 15, 42, 55, 71, 97, 110, 112, 164, 166–7, 176, 183, 188, 191–2, 198, 205, 211, 247

Cervantes, Cardinal, 41

Cervantes, Juan de (Miguel's grandfather), 14

Cervantes, Juan de (Miguel's brother), 16

Cervantes, Magdalena de (Miguel's sister), 15, 42, 55, 71, 110, 112, 165, 177, 183, 190–1, 198, 210, 211, 247

Cervantes, Miguel de, birth of, 11–12, 14 ; ancestry of, 11–12, 14–16 ; childhood of, 14–16 ; joins the Spanish army in Italy, 11–13, 18 ; takes part in the battle of Lepanto, 18–23, 41 ; as satirist of war, 21–2, 26–7, 37–8 ; love affairs of, 20, 31–2, 39–40, 83–4, 99–104, 131, 134–6 ; and *Don Quixote*, 17, 18, 21–2, 27, 33–4, 37–8, 66, 101–2, 113, 120, 160–1, 166–72, 175, 178–9, 195, 197–8, 213, 219, 226–33, 234–41, 242, 249 ; takes part in the capture of Tunis, 36–8 ; sails from Italy for Spain and is captured by Algerine corsairs, 39, 41–4, 45–8 ; captive in Algiers, 49–52, 53–8, 59–63, 64–72, 73–8, 79–81 ; his attempts to escape, 53–4, 55–8, 59–63, 64–8, 71–2, 73–8, 79, 84 ; is ransomed and returns to Spain, 79–81, 86–8, 89 ; seeks employment in vain, 89–96, 97–9 ; marries Doña Catalina de Palacios (*q.v.*), 99–104, 105–11 ; and *Galatea*, 95–6, 105–8, 130 ; as playwright, 86, 109–11, 112–13, 215–16, 236–7 ; is appointed deputy-purveyor to the Armada, 113 ; his work and troubles in this capacity, 116–120, 121–7, 128–31, 137–41 ; is appointed tax-collector, 141–143 ; is imprisoned in Seville, 148–9 ; and the sack of Cadiz, 149–52 ; is again imprisoned in Seville, 154–61 ; goes to Valladolid, 161, 162 ; and

Lope de Vega, 168–73, 215–8, 223–5, 227–33, 235–6 ; is involved in Espeleta's murder, 176–87, 188–96 ; returns to Madrid, 198 ; applies for service in Naples, 207–10 ; publishes *Exemplary* Tales, 219–223 ; last illness of, 242–6 ; death of, 247 ; burial of, 248–50

Cervantes, Rodrigo de (Miguel's father), 11–12, 14–15, 55, 71, 109–10, 199

Cervantes, Rodrigo de (Miguel's brother), 16, 40–1, 47, 50, 56, 58, 60–1, 94, 97, 110, 128

Cervantes, Maria de (Miguel's aunt), 15

Cetina, Agustin de, 142

Chacón, Francisco, 224

Charles V, Emperor, 30, 36, 38

Chaves, Cristóbal de, 160

Chaves, Rodrigo de, 86, 94

Colonna, Marco Antonio, 19

Cordoba, Vicar-general of, 123

Cordoba, Martín de, 66, 71

Cortinas, Doña Leonor de (Miguel de Cervantes' mother), 11–12, 55, 71, 80, 110, 112, 141

Council of the Indies, president of, 128–9

Cuenca, Juan de, 144

Cuesta, the printer, 167

Dali Mami, 47–8, 50–1, 53, 57, 68

Desdemona, 103–4

Díaz Carrillo de Quesada, Pedro, 45, 50–1

Dido, 36

Doria, Giovanni Andreas, 19

Drake, Sir Francis, 150

Duarte de Acuña, 11–12

Eboli, Prince of, 54

Eboli, Princess of, 54–5, 98, 152

Elicio (character in *Galatea*), 106

Elizabeth of England, Queen, 150

Escobedo, Juan de, 54–5, 90, 98

España, Alonso de, 144

Espeleta, Gaspar de, 180–7, 188–192

Espinel, Vicente Martínez, 203–4

Essex, Earl of, 149–50
Exarque, Onofre, 74–6, 79, 81, 90

Falces, Marquis of, 181–2
Félix, Jerónimo, 142
Fernández de Espinosa, Juan, 95
Figueroa, Lope de, 32, 36, 41, 94, 112
Fortuni, 90
Franca, Anna, 99–100, 131, 201–2
Francavilla, Duke of, 115
Francés, Antón, 86, 89
Freire, Simón, 145–6
Fresneda, 139

Gaitán, Doña Juana, 176, 191–2
Galbán, the notary, 181, 183–5
Gandía, Duke of, 162
García, Diego, 191
García de la Torre, Lope, 195
Garcilaso de la Vega, 224
Garibay, Esteban de, and his family, 176–8, 182–4, 186–7, 189, 191
Gaul, Amadis of, 231
Gelves, Count of, 222
Gil, Father Juan, 79–81, 84–5
Gil Polo, Gaspar, 108
" Gilder, the," 60, 62, 64–5, 75
Girón, Pedro, the Granadine, 73–4, 79
Gómez de Monsálvez, Sergeant, 56
Gómez Suárez de Figueroa, Bishop of Cadiz, 160
Góngora y Argote, Luis de, 174, 180, 209, 223, 231
Granvela, Cardinal, 40–1
Guardo, Juana de, 168
Guevara, Antonio de, 113, 121–3, 137, 141
Gutiérrez, Tomás, 109, 113–6, 131
Guzman Family, 122

Haedo, Archbishop, 60, 64, 67, 69
Haro, Diego de, 115
Haro, Luis de, 115
Hassan, governor of Algiers, 59, 62
Hassan Pasha, viceroy of Algiers, 64–9, 73, 75–81, 84
Hassan Fornaro, the Genoese, 49
Henri IV of France, 238–9

Henry of Portugal, 90–1
Hera, Pedro de la, 98
Hernando de la Vega, 56
Herrera, Fernando de, 133, 172
Howard of Effingham, Lord, 149, 173

Ibarra, Esteban de, 207–8
Ibiza, viceroy of, 61
Infantado, Duke del, 171
Isabelle of France, 238
Isunza, Pedro de, 137–41, 148–9

Jafer Pasha, viceroy of Algiers, 80
Juan, governor Hassan's slave, 59–60, 62, 66
Jupiter, 223

Kelly, Fitzmaurice, 229

Lainez, 176
Lamberto, Alonso, 228
Laredo, Antonio, 209
Latasa, Jaime de, 84
Leiva, Sancho de, 41
Lemos, Count of, 173, 207–10, 219, 221–4, 238, 242, 245–6
Leocadelo, Giovanni Francisco, 42, 71, 97, 164
Lerma, Duke of, 162, 165, 209–210
Loaysa, Archbishop, 162
Lomelin, Napoleon, 97
Lope de Vega, 87, 168–73, 215–8, 223–5, 227–33, 235–6
Lope Giner, 95
López de Hoyos, the humanist, 16, 112
López, Gregorio, 30
López, Jerónimo, 210
Louis XIII of France, 238
Luján, the actress, 217
Luther, 174

Macías, Sebastián, 182–3
Mainez, Ramón León, 129, 229
Majorca, viceroy of, 61
Maltrapillo, the Murcian, 49, 73, 77
Mami, the Calabrian, 49
Mangado, Rodrigo, 98
Manoel the Great of Portugal, 91
Márquez de Torres, the censor, 239–40

Martí, Juan José, 228
Martínez Marcilla, Father, 240, 246–7
Medina-Sidonia, Duke of, 121–2, 126, 150–1, 159, 172
Medrano, mayor of Argamasilla de Alba, 154
Méndez, Simón, 168, 177, 188, 190–2
Mendoza, Doña Juana de, 171
Meneses, Francisco de, 53
Mesa, Cristóbal de, the poet, 214
Mexias de Las Ruelas, Diego, 115
Mira de Mescua, Antonio, 208, 223
Miranda, Diego de, 176, 191–2
Molina, Luis de, 200–2, 205–6, 211–3
Montalván, Juan Pérez de, 233
Montalvo, Luis Gálvez de, 108
Montemayor, Jorge de, 108
Montoya, Doña Luisa de, *see* Garibay
Morales, Alonso de, 109
Moscoso, Francisco, 138–9
Moscoso, Melchior de, 224
Moura, Cristóbal de, 90–2
Muley Mahomet, 36
Muñoz, Pedro, judge, 191
Mustapha, 19, 22

Navarrete, Sergeant, 53, 56
Navas, Juan de las, 176
Negrón, Luciano de, 159

Ochoa, 133
Ocrato, prior of (Dom Antonio of Portugal), 91, 93, 97–8
Olivar, Father Jorge del, 60–2, 72, 90
Olmedilla, Bernando de, judge, 146
Orange, Prince of, 149
Ortigosa, Francisco de, 209
Osorio, the knight, 53, 56
Osorio, Rodrigo, 137–8
Osuna, Duke of, 115
Otalora, Alonso de, judge, 191
Othello, 103–4
Ovando, Constanza de (Miguel de Cervantes' niece), 176–7, 188, 191, 206, 211, 245–7
Oviedo, Miguel de, 128, 141

Pacheco de Portocarrero, Alfonso, 71
Pacheco, Francisco, 132–3
Padilla, Father Pedro, 35
Palacios, Doña Catalina de (Miguel de Cervantes' wife), 99–101, 103–4, 105–7, 109–10, 112, 131–2, 142–3, 148, 165–6, 168, 176–7, 202, 205–7, 211, 246–7
Palacios, Francisco de, 101, 103, 168, 206
Palacios, Juan de, 105
Palofax, Jerónimo de, 84
Paravicino, Father Hortensio Félix, 203
Pedroso, Bartolomé de, 168
Pedroso, Bernabé de, 155, 160
Periander, 157
Pérez, Antonio, 54–5, 90, 98
Philip II, 18, 29, 32, 36, 41, 54–5, 85, 89–95, 113, 118, 121–3, 125–6, 128, 130, 139–40, 146–7, 151–2, 153, 165
Philip III, 161, 162–5, 174, 228
Philip, Prince of Asturias (afterwards Philip IV), 173, 238
" Pilgrim, the " (character in *Persiles*), 13
Pinheiro da Veiga, Tomé, 135–6, 163–4, 174, 192–5
Pius V, Pope, 18
Purification, Friar Alonso of the, 184

Quevedo, Francisco de, 203, 233
Quijada (Quijano), Alonso, 101–3
Quixote, Don, see Cervantes, Miguel de

Ragio, Agustín, 177
Ramadan Pasha, viceroy of Algiers, 60
Ramírez, Doña Mariana, 176, 191–2
Ramírez de Arellano, Juan, 207
Ramírez Fariñas, Fernando, 212
Rios, Ensign, 53, 56
Rios, playhouse manager, 109
Robles, Blas de, 105
Robles, Francisco de, 166–7, 178, 198–9, 204, 221, 223, 245
Rodríguez, Alonso, 99–100
Rodríguez, Gabriel, 145

Rojas, Anna de, *see* Franca, Anna
Ruiz, Juana, 181, 184–5
Ruiz de Alarcón, Juan, 229
Ruiz Pérez de Biedma, Captain, 50, 56

Saavedra, Isabel de (Miguel de Cervantes' daughter), 83, 99, 165–6, 176–7, 188–92, 199–202, 205–6, 211–3, 246
Salas Barbadillo, Alonso Jerónimo, 203–4
Salazar Vozmediano, Fernando de, 206
Saldaña, Count of, 210
Saint John of the Cross, 135
Saint Theresa, 135, 224
Saint Thomas, 227
San Pedro, Francisco de, 20, 24–6
Sánchez de Alcaudete, 84
Sánchez, Simón, 144
Sandoval y Rojas, Cardinal-Archbishop Bernardo de, 173, 238–9, 245–6
Sannazaro, Jacobo, 108
Santa Cruz, Marquis of, 19, 34, 94, 121
Santes Ambrosio, the Florentine, 71
Sanz del Aguila, Diego, 199–200
Sanz de Saavedra, Isabel (Miguel de Cervantes' granddaughter), 199, 211, 213
Sanz de Zumeta, the poet, 151
Sayavedra, the playhouse manager, 109
Scipio, 36
Sebastian of Portugal, King, 90–91, 158
Segorbe, Duke of, 115
Selim, Sultan, 19
Sesa, Duke of, 41, 215
Shakespeare, William, 103
Silva, Francisco de, 214
Simancas, Bishop Diego de, 40
Siruela, Count of, 194
Sixtus V, Pope, 90
Soleiman the Magnificent, Sultan, 19
Soler, Pedro, 73
Sosa, Doctor Antonio de, 84–5
Soto de Rojas, Pedro, 214
Strata, Carlo, 200

Strozzi, Philip, 94
Stuarts, 174
Suárez, Gabriel, 142
Suárez de Figueroa, Cristóbal, 209, 214, 249
Suárez Gascó, Francisco, 142, 146, 203

Téllez, Doña Maria de, 194
Teves, Melchior de, judge, 191
Timbrio (character in *Galatea*), 46
Tirso de Molina, 229
Toledo, Antonio de, 59
Toledo, Fernando de, 168
Torres, 90

Uceda, Duke of, 210
Ugena, Baltasar de, 205
Urbina, Diego de, 18–19
Urbina, Juan de, 198, 201–2, 212
Uruk Bey, Persian Ambassador, 193

Valcárcel, Juan, 50
Valcázar, Juan de, 56
Valdivia, Diego de, 113
Valencia, Captain Francisco de, 56, 59
Valencia, viceroy of, 61
Valera, Juan, 142
Vallejo, judge, 147, 155
Valles, Doña Anna de, 164
Vázquez, Mateo, 32, 54–5, 89–90, 92
Vázquez Aldarete, Diego, 54
Velada, Marquis of, 162
Velázquez, Diego de, 132
Velázquez, Jerónimo, the actor, 109, 216
Vera, Rodrigo de, 11–12
Viana, 60, 62
Vicente, Francisco, 191
Villahermosa, rector of, 208
Villalón, 85
Villanueva, Marquis of, 115
Villaroel, Cristóbal, the magistrate, 182–7, 188–192
Villaroel, Juan de, the bookseller, 237, 245
Villegas, the playhouse manager, 109
Villegas, the poet, 249
Vishnu, 122
Vizcáino, Juan, 73

Yatara, Marquis of, 116